GROWING TRUE DISCIPLES

GEORGE BARNA

ISSACHAR RESOURCES
A DIVISION OF BARNA RESEARCH GROUP, LTD.
VENTURA, CALIFORNIA

Library of Congress Cataloging-in-Publication Data
Barna, George
Growing True Disciples / George Barna
00-108713
ISBN 0-9671372-3-3 Hardcover

Printed in Canada

CONTENTS

ACKNOWLEDGMENTS

This book is a collaborative effort. I designed and analyzed the research, and wrote the text of this book. My colleagues at Barna Research implemented the research process. My family and friends prayed for me during the intensive two weeks of writing this book. The church leaders who are modeling discipleship shared their experiences and insights with us. The thousands of people we interviewed about their faith and their discipleship experiences provided invaluable understanding of where the Church is today, and where we need to go. Take any of these pieces away from the puzzle and it ceases to be a puzzle, merely an incomplete collection of items that have no apparent purpose.

Let me specifically thank some individuals whose efforts on this project deserve special recognition. David Kinnaman kept Barna Research running during my absence and has been an incredible colleague to work with. I could not have abandoned the company without him so masterfully calling the shots. Rachel Ables was a constant source of encouragement and enthusiasm, supportive to the hilt. While keeping eighty three other balls in the air she also managed the editing, design, production and distribution of this book, getting it out in less than a week after I gave her the manuscript, producing books within just a few weeks of the date from when I finished the book. (And, by the way, this is the second book I have written – and she has pushed through the process - within a four-week period. "You go, girl.") The other members of the core team pulled their weight and then some during this period; they are a privilege to minister with as we strive to help the Church. Thanks are due to Pam Jacob, Jill Kinnaman, Carmen Moore, Sarah Polley, Irene Robles, Celeste Rivera, and Meg Wells.

Once again, Julie Carobini provided keen, virtual overnight editing. Kim Wilson kept the efforts of The Barna Institute, our "sister," non-profit organization that strives to support churches, progressing despite my disappearance to write this book. She, like the rest of our team, is a wonderful example of discipleship in action.

Once again, my family has been a source of joy, strength and encouragement during the book-birthing process. They endured the required sacrifices without complaining, and shared the joy of achievement upon the book's completion. To my girls – my wife Nancy, and my daughters Samantha and Corban – you know that you are the best! Thanks for loving me during a process that makes me unlovable. May this book produce spiritual fruit that more than repays your investment in me and in this process.

As a disciple of Jesus, I must save the greatest praise and thanks for Him. He directs my paths, He opens doors, He strengthens me and He loves me. I pray that this book will be an act of worship and service that He finds worthy of His name. And I pray that my life will be worthy of that name, too.

CHAPTER 1

DO YOU WANT TO MAKE A DIFFERENCE?

Most Christian churches try to have a positive impact upon society and individuals. The big question is whether what they are doing is working. If the conclusion is that their efforts are not producing the desired outcomes, then the big challenge is whether they are willing to change their strategies to maximize their potential.

If you study how Christians and Christian churches attempt to influence their world, you will find that there are all kinds of strategies and tactics in place. We try to elect politicians who share our values and goals. We strive to enact laws and policies that reflect our beliefs. We attempt to expose people to Christian ideas and precepts through religious radio and television programming. We hope to shape the minds of young people by enrolling them in Christian schools or by ensuring that God and His principles are not completely removed from the public school environment. We use clever advertising campaigns and comprehensive direct marketing programs to encourage people to attend our churches or to develop a relationship with God. We endeavor to get people to know Jesus by inviting them to evangelistic crusades, revivals or other outreach events.

All of those efforts are well-intentioned and bear some fruit for the kingdom of God. **But here's a better strategy: convert the four out of every ten adults and one out of every three teenagers who have asked Jesus Christ to be their Savior into inspired, unmistakable disciples of Jesus.** This means that we will not be satisfied with people having confessed their sins and having said a prayer inviting Jesus to be their redeemer. Instead, we use that as a launching pad for a lifelong quest to become individuals who are completely sold out – emotionally, intellectually, physically, spiritually – to the Son of God.

Churches work hard at trying to expand and strengthen the kingdom of God by engaging in all types of creative and life-affecting ministries. Thousands of churches are currently in the process of fine-tuning their worship services to make them more attractive and compelling to people. The typical church labors to integrate numerous programs, classes and other offerings into its menu of possibilities. Millions of dollars flow from church budgets into events each year in an effort to influence the thinking and behavior of people. Literally billions of dollars are spent every year maintaining, upgrading, and expanding the buildings and facilities of churches to provide the space and equipment required for the ministry planned by the church. To appeal to people who have thus far turned a cold shoulder to God, churches and denominations launch sophisticated marketing campaigns designed to reposition churches and raise awareness of the things of God.

All of those activities can be justified by their intent and outcomes. **But here's a better strategy: ignite people's passion for God and get out of their way.** When individuals are single-minded in their devotion to God, their commitment to His ways and His principles becomes much deeper, much more intense. Once they have made an enduring and serious commitment then the peripherals don't matter as much. They'll endure worship services that may not meet their exact specifications because their focus is on God, not themselves. They'll attend activities at times that are not optimally convenient because the most important reality is to experience God's presence. They will sacrifice more of their hard-earned money for the purposes of ministry because they recognize that they are managers, not owners. They will gladly share their faith in Christ with non-believers because they understand their responsibility to other people and to God, and because they simply cannot contain their own excitement about the privilege of relating to God.

If you talk to pastors, church staff and lay leaders across the nation you quickly discover that churches work hard to increase attendance figures, to provide a full range of programs and to have adequate facilities to support a broad-based, inclusive ministry. The people and resources available for such ministry efforts represent a tremendous blessing from God.

But what if we were to change our standards? Suppose we were to de-emphasize attendance statistics, square footage and income figures in favor of a commitment to depth and authenticity in discipleship? We would redefine "success" in our churches to include:

- Congregants who worship not just on Sundays but every day of the week; not just in the sanctuary but wherever they are

- Constant efforts by the laity to discover new insights into their faith and to convert that information into personal application

- Complete submission to the Holy Spirit in both decision-making and behavior

- Hearts that are sensitive to sin and wounded every time we do something that offends God

- Individuals who joyfully share their resources – time, money, skills, information, relationships, possessions – with those in need, especially those who share a love of Christ and a commitment to His people

- A deep commitment to building a lasting and life-changing community among those who profess Jesus Christ as their Savior and Lord

- Demonstrating selfless compassion toward those in need of emotional, physical, financial or spiritual assistance

- Engagement in "organic evangelism" – the process of sharing one's faith in Christ in very natural and unforced ways, based on relationships with the recipients of the information and supported by lifestyle modeling

- People who live differently than the norm because of their faith, leading lives that conform to the dictates of Scripture without cutting corners or trying to interpret biblical passages for personal comfort or advantage

- A church body that projects (and lives up to) an image of being loving, caring, focused and clear-minded in its pursuit of the ways of God.

- Individuals who are continually linked to God through prayer and meditation, as if they were "online" 24 hours a day with the ultimate spiritual power

- Believers who take the initiative to use their gifts, skills and training for the benefit of their church, without having to be cajoled into serving

Why would these outcomes constitute "success?" Because churches would be made up of true disciples, not members; churches would be bolstered by the efforts of the lay ministers with the paid professionals facilitating rather than initiating and leading those efforts.

Most church leaders will nod their heads in approval and suggest that these are the very things that they are striving to achieve in their church. In all honesty, though, few churches achieve these outcomes, largely because we're not really serious about them. If we were to redefine discipleship, and truly invest in it, we could reach these laudable ends.

What Are We About?

In this book, I want to inform you and inspire you in relation to discipleship. To pastors and staff, discipleship is a tired word. To most lay people, it is a meaningless word. If you don't like the term, substitute something else in its place each time I use it. Let's not get hung up on terminology for the moment. Let's get hung up on our failure to produce indefatigable imitators of Christ. Let's get motivated by our waning influence in the world. Let's commit to doing whatever it takes to reinvigorate the Church so that it will honor God, help to change lives, and take its rightful place as the primary agent of transformation in our culture.

How many times have you heard the Great Commission? A hundred? A thousand? Communicated in the right context, it can get your juices flowing, right? But how many people do you know whose articulated life purpose is to fulfill that tremendous challenge? How many believers do you know who get out of bed every morning and pray and think about what they can do that day to show and tell people about Jesus, to make those people disciples of the Lord, and to act like a true disciple themselves?

Here's a morsel of perspective. In one recent nationwide survey we asked people to describe their goals in life. Almost nine out of ten adults described themselves as "Christian." Four out of ten said they were personally committed to Jesus Christ, have confessed their sins and believed they were going to Heaven after they died because of God's grace provided through Jesus' death and resurrection. *And not one of the adults we interviewed said that their goal in life was to be a committed follower of Jesus Christ or to make disciples of the entire world – or even of their entire block.* (That survey, by the way, included interviews with pastors and other church leaders, as well as hundreds of people who regularly attend church services and programs.)

I want to challenge you to re-think what discipleship means and what it looks like in your church. I want you to re-evaluate how you, personally, disciple other people. I want you to reassess the nature of your own commitment to Christ – that is, your own spiritual growth. Toward that end, let me suggest that we will probably have to alter the ways in which we think about and practice discipleship. Here are some of the transitions that you and your church may have to make to improve the quality of our followership.

- ❑ Shift from a program-driven ministry to a people-driven ministry

- ❑ Change from emphasis on building consensus to building character

- ❑ De-emphasize recalling Bible stories, emphasize applying Bible principles

- ❑ Move from a concern about quantity (people, programs, square footage, dollars) to a concern about quality (commitment, wisdom, relationships, values, lifestyle)

- ❑ Retool developmental ministry efforts from being unrelated and haphazard to being intentional and strategic

- ❑ Replace ministry designed to pass on knowledge to efforts intended to facilitate holistic ministry

- ❑ Alter people's focus from engaging in the optimal feel-good activities to absolute commitment to personal growth, ministry and authenticity in their faith

Maybe you have heard such challenges before and are no longer moved by calls for revitalization. In this book I will argue that unless we embrace a comprehensive and far-reaching commitment to radical change in how we conduct our lives and our ministries, we are doomed to minimal results. If we hope to make a significant difference in the lives of individuals and in the nation's culture, then we must increase our intentionality, our intensity and improve our strategies.

An old leadership adage is relevant to our dilemma: the things that got us to where we are today will not get us to where we need to be tomorrow. Qualitative growth demands constant upgrading and intensifying of our efforts. Unless you are completely satisfied with the state of your personal spiritual life, and the spiritual life of your congregation, you must accept both the need to improve and the myriad of changes that will facilitate such improvement. Doing *more* of what you're already doing won't take you to the next level. Doing more of the same, but doing it *better*, won't get you there, either. In all likelihood, you need to integrate new strategies and new tactics to climb to a higher plane of ministry impact and lifestyle purity.

The natural tendency, of course, is to believe that we are doing okay, that we just need to tweak a few things and everything will be great. If you find yourself leaning in that direction, read the list of seven transitions again. Those are not overnight, quick-fix upgrades. Re-read the list of twelve lifestyle outcomes in the previous section of this chapter. Those are not likely to happen without some radical transitions in thinking and commitment.

It all starts with a clear sense of what you are striving to accomplish. Are you satisfied with the nature of your church today, but want it to be bigger? Or are you committed to seeing a qualitative improvement in the ministry of your church and the lives of the individuals within it?

If you understand the magnitude of what we're discussing, then you realize this is a major undertaking. Should we bother? Can't we just keep on going down the same path we're on, making incremental adjustments along the way?

No. I don't know how to state it more bluntly. The Church in America is failing to live up to its promise; we're not even coming close to fulfilling it. Our nation has a strong economy and a weak morality. People are more interested in faith and religion than they are in Jesus. Believers are largely indistinguishable from non-believers in how they think and live. The Church has lost its place at the table of cultural influence. Can we restore the impact of the Church through more events and buildings? No. It will take zealots for Christ, individuals who are intractably devoted to knowing, loving and serving Him with all their heart, mind, strength and soul, if we are to transform our world.

The Reason for Hope

Honestly, our society's only hope of moral restoration is for the Church to fulfill its calling from God. He called it into being so that the world would be impacted by the thoughts, words and deeds of His followers.

Is there any reason to believe that the Church can live up to God's mighty calling? Absolutely! In fact, there are three persuasive reasons to believe that the Church can fulfill God's lofty expectations.

First, we can look at the history of the Church. Two thousand years ago Jesus turned the world upside down by ignoring politics and institutional leverage, instead drawing twelve losers around Himself and preparing them to infiltrate the culture with a life-giving message, a transformed lifestyle and a burning desire to serve God with every ounce of capacity they possessed – or die in the process. It was an improbable strategy, but it worked. The passion of His followers was contagious. Without buildings, budgets, programs or curriculum, they built the foundations for what has become the world's most prolific faith group. America has millions of people who have accepted Christ as their savior and want their lives to have meaning and impact. Can we, the modern Church, have such impact?

Second, you must consider the heart of God. He created humans for the purpose of us knowing, loving and serving Him. His specific command to us, delivered through His Son, was that we should develop communities of faith to facilitate the developing of our relationship with Him and service to others. He equipped us for this task with special gifts and abilities, with enormous resources and, most importantly of all, His Holy Spirit that lives within and works through His followers. He gave us a huge task, yes, but He gave us all that we would need to accomplish the task. Endowed by the Creator with all the tools and resources required to shape the world into a God-fearing, worshiping community, can we master the challenge?

Third, let's not overlook one aspect of our culture that will enable us to make progress toward the desired outcome: the American can-do spirit. Americans love a good challenge. When posed with a possibility that seems just beyond our grasp but merits our energies, we often take up the cause and rise to the challenge. If God's people in the U.S. can understand what is at stake, and be given a reasonable plan of attack, it seems likely that they would energetically pursue the potential to be the true Church.

Recognize that reaching the level of excellence called for within the Church will demand three things of us. First, we must rely upon God. This is a battle we cannot win on our own strengths and abilities. We must lean heavily on His Word, His power and His guidance. Second, for the Church to be the Church He envisioned, we must commit to personal growth. That commitment intimates that we are willing to change in ways that may be uncomfortable or unexpected. Third, we must also recognize that the Church is not a private, individual endeavor but a corporate adventure. We must be willing to minimize ourselves for the good of the whole, using our abilities and resources in tandem with those of other believers for the benefit of the Church at-large.

The Picture of Success

What would success look like if the Church were to be comprised of true followers of Christ? We need only return to a well-known

15

passage of Scripture to be reminded of the product we seek to achieve.

> They devoted themselves to the apostles' teaching and to the fellowship, to the breaking of bread, and to prayer. Everyone was filled with awe, and many wonders and miraculous signs were done by the apostles. All the believers were together and had everything in common. Selling their possessions and goods, they gave to anyone as he had need. Everyday they continued to meet together in the temple courts. They broke bread in their homes and ate together with glad and sincere hearts, praising God and enjoying the favor of all the people. And the Lord added to their number daily those who were being saved. (Acts 2:42-47)

You cannot have that kind of experience unless you are fully devoted to the cause. The early disciples were sold out to Jesus and His plan – i.e. the church carrying on His teachings through their lives, and communicating them to others through their words and deeds. The early church was not about specialists employing foolproof techniques; it was about sinners receiving grace, committing to change, and living in concert with the wisdom imparted by their faith resources – i.e. the Word of God, the lives of fellow sojourners and the leading of the Holy Spirit.

Do you know anyone who wants that kind of life? Are you willing to pull out all the stops to help them have it?

Where We're Going

Discipleship is not about reading books and storing up knowledge. My objective, however, is to use this printed vehicle to provide you with information that may help you design a plan for your church and your life that will result in an Acts 2 type of experience. Here's how I hope to accomplish that outcome.

In **chapter 2** we will explore some of the nuts and bolts of discipleship – definitions, Scriptural justifications, and a framework for the journey.

In **chapter 3** I will present a brief overview of the current state of the Church – individually and institutionally – as the context within which we are serving. You cannot intelligently change reality until you understand it.

Chapter 4 will provide an analysis of how we got to our current state of reality. This chapter will help us avoid the same traps and pitfalls that got us to our current state of ineffectual spirituality.

You cannot get too far without a goal in mind, so **chapter 5** will outline the goal of discipleship. Note that this chapter is not a step-by-step plan of action for your church, since every church will be unique, but it will offer some adaptable guidelines for the development of your church's agenda.

Chapter 6 will distill for you the findings from my research among a couple of dozen churches across the nation that are doing outstanding work in the area of discipleship. You will discover the philosophies and practices that these churches have in common that are transferable to your church.

The research led me to see that there are five viable models in place in the outstanding churches. In **chapter 7** I will describe those models briefly for you with the expectation that you may want to adapt one of them to your circumstance.

The **final chapter** ties it all together and poses one last challenge to your resolve: are you really committed to being and to reproducing committed followers of Jesus Christ?

The new millennium is a tremendous time for us to focus on true discipleship. People are searching for answers, for relationships, for meaning. The Church has everything that people are seeking. If we are serious about ministering to people, we could not have asked for a better place and a better time in history to be alive. The challenges are enormous, of course, but the possibilities for incredible results are equally vast. This is a time of unparalleled potential and promise, if we are willing to pay the price to follow the Lord.

CHAPTER 2

FOCUS ON THE FUNDAMENTALS

Before we get too far down the trail, let's agree on some fundamental aspects of discipleship. We should start with a clear definition of what that term means in this book; a discussion of why it's important; and some consideration of what true discipleship looks like in practice.

What Is Discipleship?

In the original biblical texts, the term used for disciple refers to someone who is a learner or follower, serving as an apprentice under the tutelage of a master. The apostles are great examples of this relationship between a student and master: they followed Jesus, the master teacher and model of the Christian faith, striving to learn from His words and deeds, growing through the practical, hands-on training that He facilitated. Discipleship connotes that you are being prepared for a particular lifestyle more than for a specialized occupation.

We might define discipleship as becoming a complete and competent follower of Jesus Christ. It is about the intentional training of people who voluntarily submit to the lordship of Jesus Christ and who want to become imitators of Christ in every thought, word and deed. On the basis of teaching, training, experiences, relationships and accountability, we become beings transformed into the likeness of Jesus Christ.

Discipleship, in other words, is about being and reproducing spiritually mature zealots for Christ.

I believe the intensity conveyed by the word zealot is important for us to associate with discipleship. Most Christians lack a true understanding of the context within which Jesus' disciples were developed. As a result, we minimize the investment required to be a "follower." When we hear that the apostles were followers of Jesus, the image that comes to mind is of people who tagged along after the Lord on His walks through the hot, dusty towns of Israel. The followers were there to listen, to watch and to be amazed at what the Son of God did in their presence.

You and I are followers of many different people, organizations, activities and ideas. For instance, I follow the New York Yankees. When they win a game I'm happy for a few seconds and then I get on with my life. When the Yankees lose a game I'm disappointed for a few seconds and then I get on with my life. I am not a Yankee zealot – a person who is single-mindedly invested in the day-to-day fortunes of that team.

When the New Testament talks about being a follower of Jesus, consider what it meant to be in the elite group of twelve. Each of them abandoned his profession. Each man lived a minimalist lifestyle, carrying few possessions and having no enduring sense of residential stability. They learned new principles constantly, and were expected to apply those principles on demand. Because their Teacher and His ways were so radical and threatening to some of society's powerbrokers, they suffered persecution although all they tried to do was help people. Their training period was for an unspecified duration, but it lasted in excess of two years before being "prematurely" curtailed. There were no textbooks on which they could rely, so they had to be constantly alert and had to retain all of the information and insights gleaned during their training stage. In short, they had no life apart from what they were being trained to do. Being a follower of Jesus Christ was an all-consuming obsession.

The Church these days has many "followers" of Christ in the sense that I follow the Yankees: we dabble in Christianity. That's not what Jesus had in mind when He called us to become His disciples. He is seeking people who are absolutely serious about becoming anew – individuals who are fanatics, zealots, mesmerized, passionate about the cause, completely devoted to mimicking their model down to the last nuance.

> Discipleship is not a program. It is not a ministry.
> It is a lifelong commitment to a lifestyle.

How Important Is Discipleship?

My study of discipleship in America has been eye-opening. Almost every church in our country has some type of discipleship program or set of activities. Stunningly few churches have a church of disciples.

Maybe that's because it's not terribly important. If we can get people to attend worship services, pay for the church's buildings and salaries, and muster positive, loving attitudes toward each other and toward the world, perhaps that's good enough. What does the Bible have to say about the significance of discipleship?

Plenty.

We might start with a brief review of key passages regarding the nature of discipleship. Here are six Scriptural insights into the importance of discipleship.

1. Disciples must be assured of their salvation by grace alone.

Embracing the free gift of salvation made available to us through the death and resurrection of Jesus Christ initiates our journey as a disciple of Christ. Without the relationship made possible by the acceptance of His gift to us, a person cannot progress as a disciple; rejection of the cross represents an insurmountable obstacle to being a committed follower of Jesus. All human beings are invited to become true disciples of the Lord, but the terms of admission into the training program are that we confess our sins and accept Christ as our Savior. Until that score is settled, complete devotion to Christ is impossible.[1]

2. Disciples must learn and understand the principles of the Christian life.

If we are to truly own and then give away our faith, we must have a deep and complete comprehension of that faith. We live in accordance with what we know; we can only give what we ourselves possess. Therefore, it is imperative that anyone who wishes to be a disciple commit to gaining insight into the nature and substance of the Christian faith, and to work towards a total integration of the principles of that faith in his/her life. You cannot pass that faith on to others if you are not living it; and you cannot live it if you do not understand it.[2]

3. Disciples must obey God's laws and commands.

Professing allegiance to a cause is one thing; proving your allegiance through actions that are consistent with the core beliefs and practices of the cause is something else. To be a true disciple does not require perfection; if it did, there would be no Christianity existent today. True discipleship does, however, demand that an individual constantly strive to live in harmony with God's laws and commands. It is not enough to know those admonitions; a disciple is devoted to carrying them out in his/her life. The result is a lifestyle that is distinguishable from the norm: vision, values, goals, relationships and behavior that is different from the established patterns and accepted norms.[3]

4. Disciples must represent God in the world.

Followers of Jesus Christ are not given the option of telling people "do as I say, not as I do." Our lives must reflect the ways of God. But even more than that, we are to be God's ambassadors in the world. We are not called to retreat or to live in isolation, but to be light in the darkness, which requires being in the midst of that darkness. We are to be alert to opportunities to represent God in ways that honor Him. And the Great Commission is clear in telling us to pursue the world, rather than to wait for it to pursue us.[4]

5. Disciples must serve other people.

The purpose of discipleship is to become a transformed individual who will imitate Christ. Jesus' life was about selfless love of others – a life devoted to serving people. Our objective must be to become prepared to understand and address people's needs with the same love, sensitivity and skill demonstrated by Jesus during His earthly ministry. The purpose of discipleship is to become a servant; only through serving does one become a master.[5]

6. Disciples must reproduce themselves in Christ.

The end goal of disciples is both personal and corporate. The personal goal is to live a life worthy of the name "Christian." The corporate goal is to introduce other people to Jesus, enable them to adopt Him as their savior, and then to enable them to live the life worthy of someone known as a Christian. The Great Commission is not primarily about evangelism, it is about discipleship: "Therefore go and make disciples of all nations…" (Matt. 28:19) An individual who does not reproduce himself in Christ is not truly a disciple since he does not exhibit the selfless love of the Master.[6]

The viability of the Christian faith, it turns out, is intimately related to our engagement in discipleship. Jesus did not spend three years modeling the discipleship process because He wasn't sure how else to end His time on earth. The writers of Scripture did not capture Jesus' words on the meaning of discipleship and the related efforts of the apostles for lack of creative ideas. The life of the apostle Paul was not devoted to trips back and forth between the churches he started simply to gain frequent walker miles. The strength and influence of the Church is wholly dependent upon its commitment to true discipleship. Producing transformed lives, and seeing those lives reproduced in others, is a core challenge to believers and to the local church.

Living Examples

Just to make sure we did not miss the significance of discipleship as a lifestyle, the New Testament is crammed with portraits of believers engaging in discipleship. The process involves two complementary components: becoming a committed, knowledgeable, practicing follower of Jesus and instilling that same passion and capacity in the lives of others.

Consider some of the biblical samples
provided for our examination.

Jesus Christ. Jesus began His public ministry by recruiting the twelve who became known as the disciples. He spent the remainder of His time on earth pouring into them the key lessons required to understand life. His objective was to prepare them to carry on His mission in His (physical) absence. Notice how He approached discipling His followers: teaching, modeling, exhorting, encouraging. We won't do any better than to follow this process.

Paul. Nobody imitated Jesus' model better than Paul did, but his imitation is incredibly significant because he shows us that it can be done! After being saved and then discipled, he launches into an incredible time of ministry. He demonstrates the courage required to boldly represent Christ; the importance of mentoring others; and how indispensable theological knowledge and common sense are in working both inside and outside of the church.

John the Baptist. Sometimes portrayed as a quirky iconoclast, don't lose sight of John's enviable certainty and single-mindedness about his task. Before it was fashionable to be a follower of Jesus – largely because He had not yet emerged as the incarnate Son of God – John was dedicated to pointing people toward God and preparing them for the One who was to come. He was so influential that Herod beheaded him; he was so committed that Jesus went out of His way to be baptized by John; and he was so exemplary that his life story is still told to this day.

Church in Jerusalem. The first church is described for us in the book of Acts. There may be no better – and certainly no more succinct – picture of the true church than that provided in Acts 2 (see chapter 1 for the pivotal passage). It is an applied definition of discipleship: the followers of Christ engaged in worship, learning, relationships, sharing, serving, evangelizing, and prayer. The result was numerical growth, cultural influence, and the glorification of God. Their commitment exacted a price – many were persecuted and killed – but their devotion to Christ resulted in the spread of a Church that has lasted over 2000 years, regardless of the political, geographic, sociological and spiritual roadblocks that have emerged.

What we see in these examples are people who are committed to being disciples of Christ and to producing disciples of Christ – i.e., doing and facilitating. They embrace the principles Jesus taught of obeying God's commands, loving people, expressing gratitude to God through service, strategically training new followers, holding each other accountable, and working in cooperation to achieve the ends of the kingdom. Personal attitudes and behaviors are thereby changed to conform to the dictates of God.

Read through the book of Acts if you want to get excited about discipleship. It's hard to read the story of Stephen and not want to jump out of your seat and find someone to mentor. The combination of simplicity and boldness displayed by Peter is inspiring – and, given our knowledge of Peter before Pentecost, encourages us to believe that we, too, can overcome our deficiencies and weaknesses to serve the Lord with honor and impact. Following Paul on his travels throughout Asia Minor gets you both exhausted and energized. How could one man do so much in such a short period of time?

These are the stories of zealots for Christ! Because we have a glimpse into their lives prior to becoming revered saints, we know that they started off no better than us; their stories have become legendary because of their passion for the cause of Christ. Absolutely nothing was more important to them than being a disciple of Jesus Christ – and they allowed nothing to stand in the way of fulfilling that glorious opportunity.

The Marks of a Disciple

The marks of a true disciple then, are simple.

- Disciples experience a changed future through their acceptance of Jesus Christ as savior and the Christian faith as their defining philosophy of life.

- Disciples undergo a changed lifestyle, manifested through different values, goals, perspectives, activities, and relationships.

- Disciples mature into a changed worldview, attributable to a deeper comprehension of the true meaning and impact of Christianity. Truth becomes an entirely God-driven reality to a disciple. Pursuing the truths of God becomes the disciple's lifelong quest.

Take a good look at your life. Are you excited and certain about your eternal destiny, as a result of your relationship with Christ? Is your lifestyle one that you could confidently display to God without fear of criticism? Are you sufficiently conversant in the principles and purposes of your faith that give you meaning, purpose, hope and parameters?

How about your ministry to others? Do you exploit available opportunities to share your faith in Christ with those who are not believers? Are you committed to assisting any believers in pursuing personal spiritual development?

If you wonder how you're doing as a disciple, answer a few simple questions.

✓ Are you certain that your eternal salvation has been determined by your confession of sins and your acceptance of Christ's gift of forgiveness?

✓ Do you consistently obey all of Jesus' teachings?

✓ Do you always love other people, in practical ways, especially fellow followers of Christ?

✓ Have you forsaken all other attractions and distractions in this world to focus on knowing, loving and serving God?

✓ Do you carry the burdens of following Jesus with joy?

✓ Do you live in such a way as to show others what the Christian like looks like?

✓ Do you relate to other Christians consistently, in a spiritual setting and for spiritual purposes?

✓ Are you sharing your faith in Christ with those who have not embraced Him as their savior?

✓ Are you helping other believers to grow spiritually?

✓ Do you consistently seek guidance from God in all that you do?

The essence of this list is simple: you must bear fruit worthy of a follower of the risen Lord. There is no single test you will ever take that will definitively ascertain whether you are or are not a true disciple. But, as a believer, God has placed His Holy Spirit within you to enable you to discern such things. Surveys like this one are mere reminders of the importance of certain types of efforts at growing and serving. None of us would score a "perfect 10" every moment of every day; we all fall short sometimes. But as Paul instructed us, we must keep our eyes focused on the goal...

It is interesting to notice the divergent characters of the disciples. Discipleship is about becoming devoted and mature followers of Jesus, but apparently it is not about creating clones. Christianity does not require us to become bland, uniform, one-dimensional beings. We are able to maintain the idiosyncrasies and unique qualities that God bred into us. All that God wants is to transform your heart from one that focuses on self and the world, to one that beats exclusively for Him. Once that transition occurs, He will provide ways to use your distinctive qualities for His purposes.

Also realize that the disciples who started that global spiritual revolution in Jerusalem were not building the Church solely on the basis of accumulated knowledge. We must not forget that discipleship is more than learning the substance of the Bible. Stephen was obviously well-schooled in church history and was able to effectively articulate the story of the Church. But we also know that he was one of the leaders of the outreach to the needy before he was martyred. Paul was one of the world's great debaters, but we also read about his concern for the poor, the widowed and the sick. Jesus modeled this balancing of knowledge and application for His followers by dividing His time between teaching people and demonstrating love in action (e.g. healing, feeding, consoling, encouraging). Discipleship is an artful blend of what we know and what we do.

Building a Discipling Church

Discipleship cannot occur in a vacuum; it is most effectively accomplished in cooperation with other followers of the Lord. The significance of the church, as a gathering of believers, is inescapable: without the support of a body of like-minded followers, we will not reach our potential as servants of God.

My experience in studying thousands of churches across the country clearly shows that discipleship does not happen simply because a church exists. It occurs when there is an intentional and strategic thrust to facilitate spiritual maturity. Specifically, the church must have a philosophy of ministry that emphasizes the significance of discipleship, and promotes a process for facilitating such maturity. The church must provide relational opportunities for congregants, matching those who need to grow with individuals and ministries that will facilitate growth. Because serving people is such a crucial dimension of spiritual maturity, churches help people grow by giving them opportunities to meet the needs of others. One of the great – and underutilized – benefits of the church is to provide a means of accountability for those who seek to grow in Christ.

To create a discipling church takes more than having a Sunday school, small groups, or good expository preaching. As we will discuss in a subsequent chapter, churches that are most effective in discipleship have learned what is required among their people: a philosophy of ministry that places daily spiritual growth at the core of the ministry. Programs alone won't get the job done. Knowing what you're striving to produce, having a philosophy that supports that outcome, implementing a plan to accomplish the goal, and evaluating the sufficiency of the outcomes is important. Just as each believer's life is examined to see if it produces fruit, so must each church evaluate its ministry to determine the quantity and quality of the fruit it is producing.

But it all starts with a clear understanding of what we're seeking to produce: people who will be, and will reproduce, spiritually mature zealots for Christ.

Footnotes

[1] Passages regarding salvation and its relationship to discipleship include Romans 3:10-24, Galatians 3:1-5; Ephesians 1:13-14, 2:4-10; John 3:16-21; Acts 2:36-39; Titus 3:4-7; Luke 13:1-5, 22-30, 24:46-47.

[2] The importance of learning and understanding Christianity is exemplified in Matthew 6:33; Luke 14:25-35; Philippians 4:8-9; 2 Timothy 3:16-17; Hebrews 5:11-6:3; James 1:5.

[3] See Luke 10:25-28; Acts 5:29; Galatians 5:16-24; Ephesians 4:20-5:21; Colossians 3:1-17; 1 Thessalonians 4:7; James 1:22-25; 1 John 3:16-24.

[4] See John 17:14-18; Matthew 29:18; 2 Corinthians 5:20; Acts 1:8; Mark 5:18-19; Ephesians 4:1; Colossians 1:10; 1 John 2:16, 15-17; Matthew 10:16, 28:17-19.

[5] See Ephesians 2:10, 4:11-12; Matthew 16:24-28, 20:25-28; Luke 9:1-6, 10:30-37; Acts 6:1-3; Philippians 2:1-4; Hebrews 13:16; James 2:14-24.

[6] The command for disciples to reproduce themselves is found in Matthew 28:19. You can also find it in John 15:8. Other relevant passages include Matthew 9:35-38; Acts 4:1-11, 5:42, 13:47.

CHAPTER 3

THE STATE OF DISCIPLESHIP

Discipleship matters. It matters because Jesus modeled it and commanded it, because it's necessary for the Church to become healthy and productive, because we do not reach our potential without spiritual growth, and because we cannot influence the world unless we can demonstrate faith-based transformation.

How are we doing in the realm of spiritual growth? Are we fulfilling God's expectations of us? Are we avidly striving to fulfill our spiritual potential on earth?

To get a grip on this matter, let's explore a couple of areas. First, we will look at the attitudes and involvement of born again Christians in relation to personal spiritual growth.[1] Also in this chapter, we will explore the role played by the local church in motivating and supporting believers in their quest for spiritual development.

The Place of Spiritual Growth

Our research discovered an interesting condition. On the one hand, when you ask born again adults about their goals in life and give them a series of possibilities to rank, personal spiritual development emerges as one of their top priorities. For instance, four out of five believers said that having a deep, personal commitment to the Christian faith is a top priority for their future. On the other hand, when you ask believers to identify the single, most important thing they hope to accomplish in life, without suggesting any particular possibilities, only a small minority mentions anything directly related to spiritual growth (20%). In other words, most believers say that their faith matters, but few are investing much energy in the pursuit of spiritual growth.

How can these seeming contradictions be reconciled? By realizing that most born again adults acknowledge that spiritual development is a primary responsibility of a follower of Christ and may be a helpful endeavor, but that it is not a pressing need because they believe they have largely mastered the principles and nuances of the Christian faith. Most believers who say that they want to have a deep commitment to the Christian faith, but are not involved in any intentional effort to grow spiritually – and that represents three out of every five adult Christians – view their challenge to be one of spiritual maintenance rather than spiritual development. They contend that they have embraced Jesus, learned the core lessons from Scripture, and have implemented those lessons; all they need to do in the future is to continue doing what they're already doing. The one out of five believers who are actively engaged in some type of personal spiritual development activity besides attending church services are still involved in striving to learn new insights, to live in a more obedient manner, and to apply their newfound wisdom in unique and expanding ways.

How do people pursue spiritual development? The most common approaches used by those currently involved in some type of spiritual nurturing process include the following:

- two out of three (68%) are involved in a small group or cell group designed to facilitate spiritual growth;
- one out of four (24%) participate in a Sunday school class that motivates them to grow;
- one out of every seven (15%) is being spiritually mentored by someone;
- one out of every nine (11%) attends a special class for the purpose of becoming more spiritually mature.

The typical individual who allocates some energy to personal spiritual growth spends an average of four hours per week on these endeavors. Most of these people are quite regular in their commitment to spiritual growth: two-thirds invest time and energy in such matters every week, while more than four out of five growth-oriented believers engage in such activities at least monthly.

What Is "Successful Discipleship?"

Our research also points out that most born again adults are limited in their ability to grow spiritually because they have failed to set any goals for their spiritual development, to develop standards against which to measure their growth, or to have instituted any procedures for being held accountable to grow. Only four out of every ten churched believers say that they have set personal spiritual growth goals for themselves for this year.

Even that figure is inflated, though, since many of the "goals" are not measurable (i.e., "to become a better Christian" or "to grow spiritually"), not spiritual (i.e., "to be a better person") or not much of a stretch (i.e., "to attend church services"). If we recalculate the statistics on the basis of the content of their personal spiritual expectations, we find that six out of ten believers have no sense of what they want to become and roughly two out of ten have only the vaguest idea of what they might like to achieve or become spiritually. That leaves only two out of ten believers who are serious about their spiritual development and have defined rather specific goals to reach.

It is intriguing that when Christians are asked to identify their spiritual goals (see Table 3.1), few believers mentioned more than one goal that they had set for themselves. For some people that seemed to be a strategic choice – having selected only one goal made it more feasible that they would satisfy their goal or that they would not become frustrated by having too many unreachable outcomes to achieve. However, for a larger share of the goal-setters, it seemed that the paucity of personal goals reflected the absence of reflection and commitment to growth, more than a realization of the most effective path to achieving their potential.

TABLE 3.1
THE PERSONAL SPIRITUAL GOALS OF
BORN AGAIN ADULTS
(N = 417)

grow spiritually (no specifics)	26%
live a life that's more pleasing to God (no specifics)	19
be involved in spiritual growth activity (no specifics)	15
read the Bible more, know more Bible content	14
attend church more consistently	13
have a better prayer life	11
serve other people; have a personal ministry	10
participate more frequently in church activities	9
improve the spiritual state of my family	7
have good feelings about myself	2
don't remember the goals	5

(Note: percentages add to more than 100% because
people were allowed to provide more than one reply.)

These goals are further challenged by the fact that three out of ten born again adults admitted that they did not have any plan or process by which they intended to fulfill their spiritual goals. You've probably encountered this before: people who say they have set goals for their development, but who have no idea how they will go about making those goals a reality. The result is talk without action, sentiment without substance. (These types of self-deceptions lead some non-believers to label Christians "hypocrites.") The unrealistic expectations of believers – i.e., that if they have good intentions those intentions will somehow come to fruition – often leads them to wander from their faith, feeling as if God let them down or that they are not capable of spiritual growth.

In fact, when we asked a national sample of believers to describe what they would most like to accomplish in life, both positive and negative signs emerged. The data in Table 3.2 show us that there are some born again adults who center their lives around their spiritual condition, but unfortunately, those believers are few and far between. Eight out of every ten believers are more likely to court dimensions of life other than spirituality as the springboard to success and meaning. Elements such as family, career development, and financial achievement are among the emphases most likely to divert people's attention from their spiritual growth. None of these outcomes is necessarily bad or indefensible; however, the infrequent adoption of spiritual maturity as the driving focus of life suggests that to most believers, their faith is a "bonus" or an add-on dimension of their life rather than the priority around which everything in their life is built.

Half of the two out of ten who cited some type of spiritual outcome as their crowning achievement in life identified rather basic spiritual realities, such as knowing that they are saved or maintaining faith in God, as their supreme life goal. Is that all we can hope for? Is there no more to the Christian faith than accepting a free ticket to Heaven or remaining convinced that God exists? Perhaps this is why half of all born again adults, and more than two-thirds of born again teenagers, say that they are searching for meaning and purpose in life – in spite of having engaged with, and made a lifelong commitment to Jesus Christ!

TABLE 3.2
WHAT IS THE SINGLE, MOST IMPORTANT THING
YOU WOULD LIKE TO ACCOMPLISH IN YOUR LIFE?
(BASE: 450 BORN AGAIN ADULTS)

being a good parent, raising good kids, having happy kids	29%
spiritual condition: having faith, going to Heaven, doing God's will, evangelizing, raising my kids to be Christian	20
financial security, comfort, retirement funds, wealth	14
completing/furthering my education	7
making a difference in the world; helping other people	7
experiencing career success; having a good job/career	7
having good health	6
having a good marriage	4
being a good person; being known as a good person	4
having a good life: being happy; being fulfilled	3
nothing in particular	9

(Note: percentages add to more than 100%
because some people gave more than one answer.)

The information outlined in Table 3.3, regarding believers' definitions of spiritual success, provides another revealing glimpse into the minds and hearts of believers. The good news provided by the data is that believers possess a diversity of ideas regarding spiritual success; there is not a mindless recitation of a simplistic notion of success embraced by the masses. Clearly, many believers have thought about what makes them successful in God's eyes. Some of the conclusions drawn by the individuals we interviewed evidenced considerable reflection and wisdom.

The most disturbing outcomes discernible in this table, though, are how few believers seem to possess the big picture of spirituality in mind, and that very few believers (less than one out of five) described spiritual success in terms broader than a single aspect of personal maturity. Most born again adults have a very narrow view of what they are striving to become as Christians, what spiritual maturity might look like in their life, and what it would take for them to maximize their potential as a follower of Christ. The dilemma is not that believers deny the importance of spiritual growth, or have failed to consider the challenges it raises, but that they seem to have settled for a very limited understanding of the Christian faith and their capacity in Christ.

TABLE 3.3
WHAT WOULD MAKE YOU SPIRITUALLY SUCCESSFUL?
(BASE: 417 BORN AGAIN ADULTS)

following Jesus; patterning my life after His; living as He leads me	15%
having a personal/growing relationship with Jesus	15
experiencing inner peace/emotional peace	13
being blessed by God	11
having assurance of my salvation; being saved; receiving God's grace	11
believing in God	8
reading the Bible; doing what the Bible says	7
sharing my faith with other people	7
being obedient; behaving appropriately (specific examples given)	6
having a good spiritual life as a family	6
obeying the Ten Commandments; obeying God's rules	5
engaging in appropriate behavior (no specifics)	5
going to church every weekend	4
being an example to others through my lifestyle	4
being happy with life	4
helping other people	3
teaching other people about Jesus; helping others to grow spiritually	2
other (general comments)	20
don't know	14

(Note: percentages add to more than 100% because some people gave more than one answer.)

Obstacles to Maturity

Do you get the sense that believers are honestly trying to grow spiritually – but not real hard? To verify that intuition, we asked believers about the intensity of their commitment to personal spiritual growth. Not quite one out of every five (18%) said that their effort to grow spiritually is the single, most intense commitment in their life today. Half of the believers said that even though they work at spiritual growth consistently, they have not reached the level of maturity or commitment to maturity that they would like. One out of every five said they occasionally delve into spiritual development, but they are not consistent about those efforts. The remaining one out of ten believers admitted that they are neither involved nor interested in development.

HOW SERIOUS ARE BELIEVERS ABOUT SPIRITUAL GROWTH?

no effort, no interest

most serious commitment in their life

inconsistent effort, limited returns

10%

18%

20%

52%

consistent effort, limited returns

You can probably guess the reasons why believers are not more zealous about discipleship. Two-thirds said they are just too busy to give the process the time it requires. One-quarter cited a general lack of interest or motivation to grow. One-tenth said they suffer from personal limitations such as emotional or financial problems. One-tenth cited health problems as their barrier.

Does anything strike you about that list of obstacles? Essentially, all of them relate to one thing: a lack of passion to be godly. Such a deficiency raises questions as to how sincere people are about their faith, or how real their relationship is with Christ, or how they understand the values of Heaven as opposed to those of earth. One thing I have learned about people: if you want something to get done, ask the busiest person associated with your cause. They are busy because they have goals, they prioritize, and they are committed to accomplishing their goals. But what happens within the Church? We're all busy, and Jesus comes along and asks us to get serious about spiritual growth. What's our response? We give intellectual assent to the idea, but when push comes to shove, our schedules are already bloated with other, more important tasks, opportunities and responsibilities. We have passion, but it is not a passion for the matters of God.

Somehow, in spite of having heard the sermons and small group lessons time and time again, we have missed the point. Can you imagine the early church choosing a different course of action when the problem erupted pertaining to the unfair distribution of food among church widows? Instead of choosing seven disciples to focus on the distribution of food and freeing the other apostles to preach, heal and evangelize, James might have stood up and said, "OK, men, that's it. This has gotten too big, too fast. Let's get some perspective; things are just out of control. I'm outta here. Who's coming with me? Let's go back to our families, our businesses, and the simple life we knew before this church thing took off."

Or what about Peter, when he was jailed in Jerusalem for preaching in public, and released at night by the angel of the Lord with the instruction to return to preaching in the public square in the morning. After regaining his freedom do you

39

think Peter would have taken the fastest horse he could find, and ridden that beast as far and as quickly as possible from the scene of his persecution, knowing that obedience to the angel's command would have won him further confrontation and hardship?

And I think it's highly unlikely that the apostle Paul would ever have written a note to Timothy, telling his young protégé, "Don't bug me anymore. You're on your own from here on. I've got so many other things to do – cashing in on my international network of contacts, searching for a wife, getting to the Mediterranean for the summer, designing the new line of tents for the Fall – I just don't have time for you and all your whining, backbiting congregants. If you have a problem – deal with it!"

Paul endured more than you or I can even dream of because he was a zealous follower of Jesus Christ. If ever anyone had a great excuse to leave the church behind, it was Paul.

> "I have worked much harder, been in prison more frequently, been flogged more severely, and been exposed to death again and again. Five times I received from the Jews the forty lashes minus one. Three times I was beaten with rods, once I was stoned, three times I was shipwrecked, I spent a night and day in the open sea, I have been constantly on the move. I have been in danger from rivers, in danger from bandits, in danger from my own countrymen, in danger from Gentiles; in danger in the city, in danger in the country, in danger at sea; and in danger from false brothers. I have labored and toiled and often gone without sleep; I have known hunger and thirst and have often gone without food; I have been cold and naked. Besides everything else, I face daily the pressure of my concern for all the churches." (2 Corinthians 11:23-28)

Paul's consistent response to the hardships of following Christ was simple: his lifestyle and ministry reflected the essence of who he was, therefore he would never give up but stay committed to obeying his calling and way of life regardless of the earthly circumstances or consequences. When human logic dictated a severe change of course, Paul persevered for one reason: his passion for God. He believed there was no way that he could outsmart God, out-give

40

Christ, or outmaneuver the Holy Spirit. When you read his story you realize there isn't anything that guy would not have done for his Lord.

The Role of the Church

Our research shows that churches have a tremendous opportunity to facilitate deeper commitment among believers. Most born again adults (95%) acknowledge that their church encourages spiritual growth. Only half of the believers we interviewed felt that discipleship is one of the two or three highest ministry priorities of their church; the other half said it is just one of many ministries or programs at their church.

The spiritual growth of millions of believers is hindered by the lack of detailed assistance and guidance provided to people who are open to being discipled. Relatively small numbers of born again adults said that their church gives them the specific paths to follow to foster such growth. Slightly less than half said their church had identified any spiritual goals, standards or expectations for the congregation during the past year. (For many people, the goals and expectations related to exhortations at the end of sermons to go forth and live in accordance with the points in the sermon. There was no personalization or other, more detailed guidance provided in many churches.) Only one out of every five believers stated that their church has some means of facilitating an evaluation of the spiritual maturity or commitment to maturity of congregants.

While many believers were more than a bit cautious about the possibility, nine out of of ten believers said that if their church identified specific changes for them, personally, to pursue in the pursuit of spiritual growth, they would at least listen to the advice and follow aspects of it, if not all of the recommendations. Very few people (5%) said they would flat-out ignore the advice. Only one out of every one hundred believers said that they would leave the church if it tried to deliver such an analysis. (Let me emphasize that this relates to congregant-specific advice for growth, not general, congregation-wide exhortations or pronouncements.)

A majority (55%) of the adults who indicated their interest in hearing advice on how to improve their spiritual life also said that if the church matched them with a spiritual mentor or coach, they would be more likely to pursue the changes suggested to them. Only 7% said that a mentor or coach would make them less likely to pursue the growth suggestions.

As noted in the previous chapter, discipleship is not a solo adventure; it is interpersonal in nature. And, like it or not, people are more likely to grow spiritually when their church is intensely and unswervingly focused on bringing people to maturity in Christ. Such an outcome is not easy to achieve – but it is paramount for the spiritual advancement and health of the individual and of the Church.

Believers are open to a variety of approaches to helping them grow. We asked born again adults to rate their likelihood of participating in each of eleven different formats of personalized training. The data in Table 3.4 show that of the eleven options, there is no "big winner" – even the most popular option was attractive to only one-third of the believers. However, there is substantial interest among believers in doing something that will take them to the next level spiritually. More than four out of five born again adults chose at least one of the eleven alternatives and said they would definitely take advantage of that possibility if it were available at their church.

One of the intriguing findings is that the most appealing options were those that are the least emotionally and personally intrusive. For instance the top six options all required very little personal revelation: a devotional guide, a weekly prayer meeting, a self-guided topical study, a group service project, a worship event and a classroom event. The high-intensity options, such as mentors, accountability partners, online chats, were farther down the list of appealing means. The implication is that many individuals in the church may be scared by the possibility of opening up their life to others and having it analyzed by outsiders. Building trust is undoubtedly one of the key factors involved in developing a viable discipleship strategy.

TABLE 3.4
THE SPIRITUAL GROWTH ACTIVITIES IN WHICH
BELIEVERS WOULD "DEFINITELY" PARTICIPATE
(N=465)

---

using a monthly devotional booklet to guide you through morning devotions	34%
participating in a weekly prayer meeting with people from your church	26
using an outline of the weekend's sermon for further Bible study on the topic	25
participating in a monthly community service project undertaken by your church	24
attending an additional worship service, either on a weeknight or weekday morning	22
attending a teaching event at your church, one night per week	19
having a weekly meeting with a mentor and three or four other people	18
having an accountability partner to meet with regularly for mutual support	17
participating in a weekly online chat room about Bible principles and applications	14
participating in a class, meeting weekly for one year, on Bible principles	14
enrolling in a seminary-level Bible teaching course, conducted online or via correspondence	12

Coaching the Saints

One of the under-utilized tactics for spiritual growth in churches is that of coaching. The idea of coaching or mentoring has been quite popular in business and educational circles for the past few years. In fact, half of all born again adults said they had received some mentoring through their church; four out of ten had received mentoring in connection with their job; and three out of ten had benefited from a mentoring process at a school.

Mentoring has influenced the lives of more than forty million adult believers; half of all born again adults claim to have been mentored or coached, in something other than sports, during their adult life. Here is what they have been coached at:

- 82% - professional or job-related skills
- 68% - religious beliefs and Bible knowledge
- 66% - how to integrate your faith into your lifestyle
- 65% - personal character traits
- 61% - relational skills
- 50% - parenting skills and perspectives
- 41% - personal finances

Mentoring may be a scary proposition to some people. It implies personal openness to evaluation, willingness to consistently work on areas of weakness, and submission to the guidance of someone else. However, an overwhelming proportion of the believers who have been mentored as an adult have positive feelings about their experience. Three out of ten said the coaching they had received was "life changing." Six out of ten said it had been "very helpful." One out of ten were less enthusiastic, citing it as having been "of some value." Only 1% of the adult believers who had been mentored said it was not helpful to them.

Our research revealed another important insight: past positive experiences in mentoring do not automatically produce believers who are anxious to be mentored in the future. Even though nine out of ten believers assigned high ratings to the value of their past experience when mentored, only one out of every seven adults said they are very interested in being mentored now or in the near future. Another one-quarter were somewhat interested in the possibility. Why the apparent change of heart? First, most churched adults are busy. Being mentored is a time-consuming, energy-depleting commitment. More people are looking to simplify their lives than are seeking to add more time pressures. Second, participation in coaching requires admission of incompleteness or immaturity. People do not lightly admit to deficiencies. Third, effective coaching requires that the student accept the expertise, the motives and the style of the coach - all elements of trust.

The research also highlighted another valuable insight. The types of people most open to being mentored were believers in their twenties, blacks, residents of the West, and upscale individuals. Why these groups? The twenty-somethings typically feel that they lacked adequate parenting, and that they have been widely rejected by authority figures and older adults. Mentoring represents an opportunity for them to receive the support they feel they were never given. Blacks have a multi-generational, community-based culture in which passing on information, skills, perspectives and encouragement is part of being black. People living in the West are notoriously open to the current fads and trends – of which mentoring is certainly one. Upscale individuals tend to have greater occupational responsibility and challenges than other people, and are thus open to learning things that will enhance their professional capacity and status. Mentoring staged a comeback in the U.S. during the past decade in the business world, as more and more corporate executives discovered the value of having an expert stand alongside them and accelerate the speed and depth of their learning curve.

Unfortunately, the bulk of people's interest in being mentored does not relate to spiritual development. The biggest category of interest was religion: 12% said they wanted to be coached to grow spiritually, and another 27% mentioned wanting to have some type of religious or spiritual mentoring occur.[2] The most popular alternative categories of interest to people included finances (15%), job or career development (12%), educational achievement (8%), parenting (8%), self-improvement (7%), and relationship building (6%).

Would church people entertain the idea of being mentored by someone they trust for the purposes of spiritual development? Yes. Three-quarters of the born again adults said that if they had that opportunity it would be very valuable; two-thirds claimed it would be exciting. Half of the believers said it would be an answer to prayer. Intriguingly, half also said being mentored spiritually would be a risk, but one worth taking. Small numbers of believers said such an activity would be too time consuming (26%), not worth the effort (18%), uncomfortable (17%), and threatening (6%).

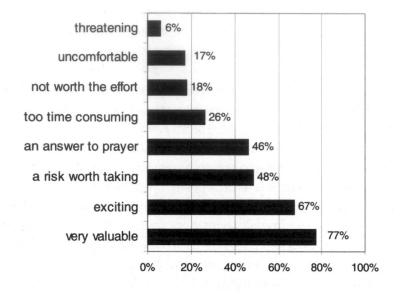

How Born Again Adults Would Feel About Working With A Mentor on Spiritual Development

What Does It All Mean?

The barrier is not that people do not have the ability to become spiritually mature, but that they lack the passion, perspective, priorities and perseverance to develop their spiritual lives. Most Christians know that spiritual growth is important, personally beneficial and expected; few attend churches that push them to grow, provide the resources necessary to facilitate that growth; or have relationships that hold them accountable for spiritual development. In the end, it boils down to personal priorities – and for most Christians, regardless of our intellectual assent to the importance of growth, our passions lie elsewhere, and our schedule and energy follow those passions.

Most believers, it turns out, are satisfied to engage in a process without regard for the product. A majority of those who say they are involved in some type of discipleship activity, for instance, contend that because they are involved in a small group, they are on track. Unfortunately, our research shows that most small groups do well with fellowship, but falter when it comes to facilitating transformation. Even the teaching delivered in most small groups has little enduring influence in the lives of group participants. Few believers, regardless of the route they select to generate growth, have goals, and most of the goals that have been set are either vague or elementary.

Churches have done a good job of promoting the importance of spiritual maturity, but have lagged in providing an environment in which spiritual growth is a lifestyle. Rather than enable maturity to become a natural extension of one's spiritual journey, it has become the exception to the rule, the domain of the spiritual superstars and fanatics. This is partially attributable to the focus on providing programs, rather than creating relationships that support growth. Although there is openness to the use of spiritual coaching, relatively few people are currently engaged in a mentoring relationship, and our interviews with churches indicate that few churches are intentionally raising up mentors and strategically matching them with congregants.

There is a tremendous need for a more intentional focus on the discipleship process and for definition to the desired outcomes of such a process. Given the proper motivation, it seems that most believers would be willing to commit to a more demanding regimen of spiritual development.

Footnotes

[1] Throughout this book, as in all of the research conducted by the Barna Research Group, the term "born again Christian" will be used to denote people who have made a personal commitment to Christ that is important in their life, and who believe they will have eternal life because they have confessed their sins and have accepted Jesus Christ as their Savior. We do not ask people to define themselves as born again, nor whether they have had a "born again experience." Instead, after people respond to the two survey questions regarding personal commitment to Christ and what they believe will happen to them after they die, we categorize the individual as born again or not born again. As of this writing, four out of ten adults and one out of three teenagers fit the born again classification. Of course, only God truly knows who is and is not a Christian. The use of

such research questions is not to condone or condemn people, but to provide an estimation of what is happening in our culture and within the Church.

[2] The people groups most desirous of such input were people in their thirties, those living in the South and Midwest, blacks, and people who are registered to vote.

CHAPTER 4

LIVING THE CHRISTIAN LIFE

Jesus was unequivocal about the importance of living differently as a result of embracing the Christian faith. The theme of His teaching and modeling was clear: "Let your light shine before men that they may see your goods deeds and praise your Father in Heaven."[1] His encounter with the rich young man cautioned His followers that being "mostly obedient" doesn't cut it.[2] He emphasized that the most important commands were to completely love God and other people.[3] He rejected the acquisition of titles, authority and worldly honors in favor of humility.[4] He extolled His followers to be servants who remain oblivious to recognition or compensation.[5] The Sermon on the Mount was a collection of challenges to behave in ways that radically departed from the norm but honored God.[6] His own lifestyle exemplified the ways in which He expects us to live: with passion, zeal and purity.[7] It was consistently demonstrated through His love and service to those He encountered, from the disciples and the crowds, to the woman at the well and Nicodemus the Pharisee – all of whom were clueless, yet all of whom were transformed by their interaction with Him.

How well do we, the Christian community in America, measure up to the example set for us by Jesus Himself, and later by the disciples in Jerusalem? To evaluate this matter, let's explore how well we're doing in regard to the pillars of church life: worship, evangelism, discipleship, stewardship, service and fellowship.[8] These are the components of the true Church, as described in Acts and modeled by Jesus in His ministry. To be true disciples, then, we ought to be growing in each of these dimensions.

Worship

There are two ways to measure our interaction with worship. The simplest and most common way is to evaluate attendance at worship services. The data show that in a typical weekend, about two-thirds of all believers attend worship services at a church. In a given month, about four out of five born again adults attend worship events. Throughout the year just less than nine out of ten believers attend at least one worship service.

The more challenging evaluation relates to people's experience at worship events. Our studies show that 14% of adult believers admit that they have never experienced the presence of God; 14% have experienced His presence, but not in the past year; and that 72% have encountered God in a real way within the past year. In a typical worship service, about half claim that they did not experience God's presence or feel as if they interacted with Him in a personal way.

Less than one-quarter of all born again adults consciously strive to make worship part of their lifestyle. For most people, worship implies attending a church service that includes music and preaching.

An underlying issue that must ultimately be resolved is the widespread ignorance among born again adults regarding the meaning of worship. When we asked people to describe the meaning of worship, 42% of all adult believers were unable to provide a substantive or reasonable reply. Among the believers who gave a substantive answer, many gave answers like "attending church" or "listening to the sermon." In total, 58% gave us a reasonable response.

When born again adults conveyed the most important outcome they want to achieve in this life, less than 1% mentioned praising and worshiping God. Few individuals deny the importance of worship; but relatively few understand what that means and have a passion to engage God through worship.

Keep in mind, by the way, that slightly more than four out of every ten adults who attend Protestant church services on a typical weekend are not born again. Their knowledge of worship – as well as each of the other pillars we are examining – is less advanced than that of the believers who occupy the sanctuary.

TABLE 4.1
THE RELIGIOUS PRACTICES OF ADULT BELIEVERS
(N=882)

in a typical week:
prayed to God	97%
had a private quiet time/devotional time	77
attended a worship service	63
read the Bible, other than at church	62
attended a Sunday school class	33
volunteered at the church	32
attended a small group/cell group	30

in a typical month:
read the Bible, other than at church	75
donated money to the church	73

in the past year:
donated money to a Christian church	84
shared faith with a non-Christian	55

in past two years:
served as a church leader/teacher	30

Evangelism

Slightly more than half of the believers (55%) claim that, during the past year, they have shared their faith in Christ with non-believers in the hope of seeing some become followers of Jesus. While the research shows that a small percentage of them are aware of anyone with whom they have shared actually choosing to follow Christ, the fact that a majority of believers claims to have engaged in evangelism represents the highest level of involvement we have seen since the early Nineties. What makes the widespread evangelism claims suspect, though, is that the figure contradicts people's attitudes about evangelizing. Less than half of all believers (46%) felt strongly that they have a responsibility to communicate their faith to non-believers. (This, by the way, represents a significant decline from a decade ago. Millions of born again adults have been influenced by the cultural cry for tolerance and acceptance of diversity related to personal beliefs and behaviors.)

No matter what the actual figure of evangelizers may be, most of the faith-sharing believers deserve credit for having evangelized non-Christians in spite of feeling that evangelism is not their spiritual gift. Only 1% of all adult believers contend that they have the spiritual gift of evangelism.

Most Christians have ample room for development in this dimension. Indisputably, evangelism is not a priority for most Christians. Less than one out of ten say that they have ever intentionally built a relationship with someone in the hope of being able to lead the person to Christ. Fewer than one out of every five believers claimed that they know a non-Christian well enough to share their faith with that individual in a context of trust and credibility. And even though a large majority of believers contends that Christians and churches should share their religious beliefs with others, only 4% lists sharing their faith with non-believers as the most important outcome they want to accomplish in their life. This, in turn, is probably related to the fact that only one out of every eight adult believers feels adequately prepared to effectively share his/her faith.

We can add to our perspective on evangelism by listening to the people who represent our local mission field. In surveys we recently conducted among large national samples of unchurched people we learned that most of them have never been invited to a church by a Christian and that most of them have never been told by a Christian what it means to be a believer in Jesus Christ, or invited to embrace Jesus as their Lord and Savior.

Discipleship

In addition to the information communicated in the previous chapter regarding discipleship and spiritual maturity, let's summarize the commitment of believers to knowing God's truths and principles.

Almost all believers own a Bible (99%); in fact, more than three-quarters of them own three or more Bibles. Most of them read from the Bible, other than during church services, in a typical week. Three out of four believers indicate that during a typical week they have at least one "quiet time" or private devotional time.

Most Christians take the Bible seriously. One-third believes that the Bible is the actual word of God and should be interpreted literally. Half perceive it to be the inspired word of God, completely accurate but containing some symbolism. One-eighth also believe the Bible is God's inspired word, but believe that it includes factual and historical errors. The remaining 5% contend that the Bible is interesting self-help literature, but not of God.

HOW CHRISTIAN ADULTS
VIEW THE BIBLE

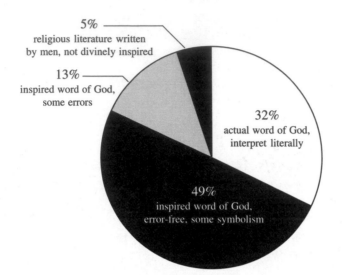

5%
religious literature written
by men, not divinely inspired

13%
inspired word of God,
some errors

32%
actual word of God,
interpret literally

49%
inspired word of God,
error-free, some symbolism

Many believers add to their Bible knowledge through the insights gleaned from public teaching events, such as Sunday school classes, small group meetings and the sermons delivered in worship services. Not quite half of all born again adults participate in either a small group or a Sunday school class during a typical week.

There is reason to be concerned about what believers claim the Scriptures teach. Take a few minutes to examine the statistics contained in Tables 4.2, 4.3 and 4.4. You will find that while many born again adults possess biblically accurate perspectives, indefensibly large numbers of believers also maintain views that are nothing short of heretical. At best we can say that most Christians hold theological beliefs that are erratic.

TABLE 4.2
WHAT CHRISTIANS BELIEVE ABOUT GOD, SCRIPTURE AND POWER

Beliefs About the Bible

	appropriate reply	percentage
It's totally accurate in all of its teachings	strongly agree	60%
The Bible teaches that God helps those who help themselves	strongly disagree	20

Beliefs About Deity and the Trinity

	appropriate reply	percentage
God is the all-knowing, all-powerful, perfect creator of the universe who still rules the world today	strongly agree	92
When He lived on earth, Jesus Christ committed sins	strongly disagree	63
After he was crucified and died, Jesus Christ did not return to life physically	strongly disagree	60
The Holy Spirit is a symbol of God's presence or power, but is not a living entity	strongly disagree	38

Beliefs About Spiritual Power

	appropriate reply	percentage
The universe was originally created by God	strongly agree	95
All of the miracles described in the Bible actually took place	strongly agree	81
Angels exist and influence people's lives	strongly agree	64

Source: Barna Research Group, Ltd, Ventura, CA. Based on national surveys of 1000 or more randomly sampled adults 18 or older, conducted July 1999 through July 2000.

55

TABLE 4.3
WHAT CHRISTIANS BELIEVE ABOUT SIN, EVIL AND SALVATION

Beliefs About sin, evil and salvation

	appropriate reply	_percentage_
All people will be judged by God after they die, regardless of their beliefs....................................	strongly agree	90%
The whole idea of sin is outdated....	strongly disagree	86
After death, some people are reincarnated – they return in another life form............................	strongly disagree	69
There are some crimes or sins people commit that God cannot forgive...	strongly disagree	60
All people experience the same outcome after death, regardless of their spiritual beliefs.................	strongly disagree	56
People who do not consciously accept Jesus Christ as their savior will be condemned to hell....	strongly agree	53
If a person is generally good, or does enough good things for others during their life, they will earn a place in Heaven...........	strongly disagree	49
You have a personal responsibility to tell other people your religious beliefs.............................	strongly agree	46
The Devil, or Satan, is a not a living being but is a symbol of evil........	strongly disagree	43

Source: Barna Research Group, Ltd, Ventura, CA. Based on national surveys of 1000 or more randomly sampled adults 18 or older, conducted July 1999 through July 2000.

TABLE 4.4
WHAT CHRISTIANS BELIEVE ABOUT LIFE

Beliefs About life

	appropriate reply	*percentage*
It is important to you to experience spiritual growth............................	strongly agree	86%
It is more important to please God than to achieve success or acceptance.....................................	strongly agree	77
You are certain that God wants you, personally, to help the poor..........	strongly agree	62
You can lead a full and satisfying life without pursuing spiritual maturity...	strongly disagree	56
All religious faiths teach the same basic principles............................	strongly disagree	53

Source: Barna Research Group, Ltd, Ventura, CA. Based on national surveys of 1000 or more randomly sampled adults 18 or older, conducted July 1999 through July 2000.

In relation to many core teachings or central beliefs, millions of believers are sorely deluded in their interpretation of what the Bible says. This situation would be a simple matter of correction if the delusions were limited to just a few aspects of Scripture, such as salvation or righteousness. However, the figures show that huge proportions of Christians – in some cases, even majorities of them – possess views that are exactly the opposite of what the Bible teaches. In summary, here is what adult Christians believe:

Three-quarters or more believe:
- the Bible teaches that "God helps those who help them selves"

- Jesus was born to a virgin
- God is the all-knowing and all-powerful perfect Creator of the universe who stills rules the world today
- the universe was created by God
- the miracles in the Bible all happened
- all people will be judged by God
- sin is not an outdated concept

For the most part, these levels of agreement with biblical teaching, while far from perfect, are encouraging. The most distressing item in this list, of course, is the fact that most Christians claim God helps those that help themselves – the antithesis of biblical truth. As fallen creatures who receive what they have by the grace of God, we are incapable of helping ourselves. It is only our arrogance and self-absorption that causes us to believe that God allows us to determine our reality and that He will simply play along.

Between half and three-quarters believe:
- the Bible is totally accurate in all that it teaches
- Jesus did not commit sins on earth
- Jesus had a physical resurrection
- the Holy Spirit is not a living entity, but just symbolic
- angels exist and influence people's lives
- people are not reincarnated
- people who do not accept Christ as Savior will go to Hell
- a person can earn entry into Heaven
- Satan is not a living entity, but just symbolic
- life is incomplete without spiritual maturity

It is at this level that the belief structure of many believers gets scary. What does it say when one-third doubt the veracity of the Bible? What do we do about the fact that four out of ten believers contend that Jesus committed sins? When more than one out of four believers reject the notion of Jesus having a physical resurrection, or a majority claim that there is no such thing as the Holy Spirit or as Satan, how healthy is the Church? When a majority says that a good person can earn his/her way into Heaven through good deeds, how much progress have we made in helping people to understand God's ways and our place in the universe?

Between one-quarter and one-half believe:
- some sins cannot be forgiven by God
- everyone experiences the same outcome after death, regardless of their beliefs
- they have a responsibility to evangelize
- all religious faiths teach the same lessons

What kind of God does one-third of all believers serve who is unable to forgive particular sins? Why believe anything at all if we all experience the same outcome after death? Why associate with Christianity if it teaches the same lessons taught by every other faith group?

To place this in yet a different context, when we asked believers for their views on 13 of these items, we discovered that only 1% of the born again adults had both a firm and biblically-consistent opinion on all 13 of the statements tested.[9] This is further evidence that believers typically possess a mixture of accurate and inaccurate views on what the Bible teaches.

In addition to these beliefs, we may examine the perspective of believers regarding the most fundamental belief of all: whether or not absolute moral truth exists. Our country is a nation immersed in moral anarchy today largely because Americans have abandoned our historic acceptance of moral virtues and absolutes emanating from the Bible. These days we are more likely to reject absolute moral truth in favor of relativism, opening the floodgates for a top-to-bottom redefinition of our most important values, attitudes and behaviors. The rejection of moral absolutes is largely responsible for undermining the health and stability of American society. The shift has occurred largely because believers have fallen asleep at the wheel.[10] Our failure to recognize absolute truth as the cornerstone of a viable worldview, and to defend it against the attack of modernism and post-modernism, has resulted in each individual becoming their own arbiter and standard of truth.

Presently, less than half of all born again adults (44%) are convinced that there is absolute moral truth. The majority of American Christians either believes or yields to the belief that all moral truth is relative to the individual and his/her circumstances. Most believers either hold a weak belief that absolute truth exists (5%), that all truth is relative (13%), or admit that they don't know what they think about moral absolutes (38%). The confusion of Christians regarding truth is verified by other research we have conducted in which we ask about truth in different ways. The outcome is a series of inconsistent views, largely because so few believers have truly grappled with the matter. This incredible confusion about

CHRISTIANS ARE CONFUSED ABOUT MORAL TRUTH

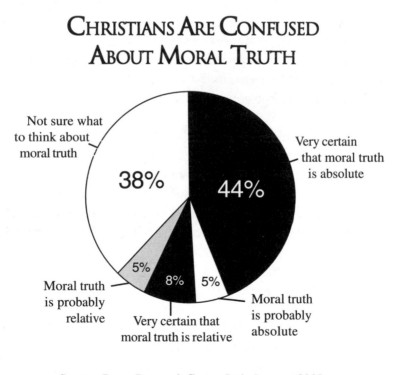

Not sure what to think about moral truth

38%

Very certain that moral truth is absolute

44%

Moral truth is probably relative

5%

8%

5%

Very certain that moral truth is relative

Moral truth is probably absolute

Source: Barna Research Group, Ltd.; January 2000;
N=417 born again Christians.

truth is at least partially attributable to the fact that only half of all believers (55%) claim that the primary influence on their thinking about moral truth is the Bible or the religious teaching they receive. The other half indicates that family and friends, experiences and observations, emotions and intuition, and other sources provide the greatest influence on their truth perspectives.

Our waffling on truth has cost us dearly in terms of ministry. In evangelism, millions of believers convey a misleading form of Christianity to non-believers, while many others delude themselves into believing evangelism really is not that critical since there are various paths to spiritual righteousness. Personal spiritual growth seems less compelling because the need for personal transformation is less imperative; for the most part, we are pleased with the way we are, and see a need for minor enhancements, at best. Absent certainty about moral absolutes, we are reluctant to "impose" our views of truth and righteousness on others; after all, it's a free society and people believe different things. And, of course, without a conviction that God is perfect, omnipotent and cares about our faithfulness to His commands, worship becomes just another option in our schedule and behavior.

Stewardship

While we could discuss true stewardship – i.e., the management of all of the resources God has entrusted to us on His behalf and for His purposes – let's limit this discussion to how well we manage the financial resources He has provided to us.

In the early Church it appears that many of the believers were poor or working class. In America these days Christians have wealth equal to that of the non-Christian segment of the population. The issue is what we do with the blessing.

Intellectually, we believe that the primary reason God has blessed us is to enjoy life and achieve personal fulfillment. There are very few believers who, without prompting, believe that we have been blessed to be a blessing to others.[11]

If we explore what we do with our finances, we find that believers frequently donate money to their church, but they don't donate too much. Three out of four born again adults give money to their church in a typical month; almost nine out of ten contribute to their church during the year. The issue is that the average total donations to churches over the course of the year was just $500 in 1999.[12] That was two-thirds of all of the money the typical believer donated to all churches and non-profit organizations during the year, but represents a small fraction of the income of believers.

Most amazing of all was the fact that only 8% of all believers tithed last year. In fact, twice as many believers gave nothing to their church last year as gave 10% or more of their income.[13]

Service

Christians may serve the Lord in many different ways. We know that one-third of them volunteer at their church in a typical week, where many of them serving as lay leaders or teachers. Half of all believers volunteer at their church at some time during the year; half do nothing in the service of their church or other people throughout the year.

A related issue concerns people's spiritual gifts. Scripture tells us that God entrusts special abilities to His people to accomplish His ends on earth. Every believer is given one or more spiritual gifts for the purpose of serving Him more completely and more capably.[14] Most believers (85%) have heard of spiritual gifts. Among those who aware of gifts, however, one-quarter does not believe that God has been true to His promise and given them, personally, a spiritual gift. Among all born again adults, then, half of them either do not know what it is or claim God did not give them a gift, one-quarter mentioned "gifts" that are nowhere to be found in the Bible, and one-quarter listed legitimate gifts they believe they possess.

When it comes to serving the poor, believers are more likely than non-believers to devote their time and energy to helping the disadvantaged of our society. Thirty-eight percent of born again adults gave time to help the poor in the past year. Forty-four percent gave some money to poor people or to organizations helping the poor. Overall, just one out of every three born again adults gave both time and money to helping the poor in the past twelve months.

Our Witness to the World

In a comprehensive study we conducted in 1997, we compared the beliefs, attitudes, values and behaviors of believers and non-believers. After studying 131 different indicators of who we are as people, we concluded that it is difficult for non-Christians to understand Christianity since few born again individuals model a biblical faith. While there are instances in which believers are different than non-believers, when we compare the two groups, the statistical differences - when they exist - are minimal. To the naked eye, the thoughts and deeds (and even many of the religious beliefs) of believers are virtually indistinguishable from those of non-believers. (To give you some perspective on statistical interpretation, realize that a difference of six percentage points is "statistically significant" – but, in real terms, that difference is invisible. It is not until you have a twenty-point difference between the two groups that the distinction begins to become noticeable, and not until you have about a forty-point difference that the gap becomes truly challenging to people and influential in their choices.)

Our research enables us to evaluate the differences between Christians and non-Christians on 42 variables regarding our non-religious attitudes and values. Among those 42 factors, we discovered that in relation to more than half of the items tested (22 items) the two groups were statistically identical or quite similar. (These are shown in Table 4.5.) On more than one-third of items (15 factors) the groups were statistically different but, in practical terms, equivalent (by which I mean less than a twenty-point divergence). (See Table 4.6 to understand these differences.) That leaves five attributes on which Christians are substantially different from non-Christians. Those attributes related to the acceptability of pornography, profanity and abortion; the need to "bend the rules" to get by in life; and the rejection of absolute moral truths. (Table 4.7 displays these factors.)[15]

Finally, regarding non-religious behaviors that would be impacted by one's spiritual commitments, we examined 15 such activities. Of those, nine were statistically identical and six showed statistically significant but pragmatically invisible distinctions. The remaining factor emerged as a visible difference: Christians were notably less likely to drink alcoholic beverages than were non-Christians. (These statistics are displayed in Table 4.8.)

TABLE 4.5
CHRISTIANS AND NON-CHRISTIANS POSSESS MANY IDENTICAL OR VERY SIMILAR ATTITUDES, OPINIONS AND VALUES

indicator	Christians	Non-Christians
your family is very important to you..............	97%	96%
you, personally, have a responsibility to share what you have with others who are poor or struggling....................................	91	86
the important thing in a relationship is not how much time you spend together but the quality of the time spent together..	90	91
you have developed a clear philosophy about life that consistently influences the decisions you make and the way you live...	84	81
your friends are very important to you..........	81	73
God helps those who help themselves..........	80	83
one person can really make a difference in the world these days.....................................	74	71
there is no such thing as absolute truth; two people could define truth in totally conflicting ways but both could still be correct..	67	76

TABLE 4.5 (CONTINUED)
CHRISTIANS AND NON-CHRISTIANS POSSESS MANY IDENTICAL OR VERY SIMILAR ATTITUDES, OPINIONS AND VALUES

indicator	Christians	Non-Christians
America is a Christian nation............................	65%	66%
nothing can be known for certain except the things you experience in your own life..	61	64
overall, you are very satisfied with your life these days..	59	52
no matter how you feel about money, it is still the main symbol of success in life.......	51	54
death penalty should be mandatory for committing premeditated murder.................	47	47
you are still trying to figure out the meaning or purpose of your life.................................	36	47
freedom means being able to do anything you want..	35	42
it's almost impossible to be a moral person today...	27	33
you favor the idea of doctors who perform an abortion being sentenced to prison for murder..	27	20
whatever is right for your life or works best for you is the only truth you can know......	26	35
you can usually tell how successful a person is by examining what they own....................	19	20
the moral and ethical standards of Americans these days are just as high as ever.............	17	25
sometimes it feels like life is not worth living	16	20
it's better to get even than to get mad...........	12	17

Source: Barna Research Group, Ltd., Ventura, CA;
1997 data, national samples.

TABLE 4.6
ON SOME ITEMS, CHRISTIANS AND NON-CHRISTIANS ARE STATISTICALLY DIFFERENT – BUT, PRACTICALLY SPEAKING, THE GAP IS INVISIBLE

indicator	Christians	Non-Christians
you favor allowing students to pray in public schools, on a voluntary basis.............................	93%	74%
parents are most responsible for teaching kids about forgiveness.................................	84	71
people are basically good.................................	79	89
when it comes to morals and ethics, or what is right and wrong, there are no absolute standards that apply to everybody in all situations	70	81
the main purpose of life is enjoyment and personal fulfillment.................................	53	66
you favor making it illegal to distribute movies or magazines that contain sexually explicit or pornographic pictures.................................	51	37
when it comes right down to it, your first responsibility is to yourself.................................	41	59
you favor the idea of couples being able to get divorced without going through the courts, but by filing notarized papers showing their intent.................................	37	55
best way for public schools to handle matters related to birth control and sex education among students under the age of 18:		
- teach sex education, promote abstinence	36	23
- teach sex education, abstinence as an option	21	20
- teach sex education, condoms/B.C. available	15	36
- leave sex educ. to parents, no condoms/B.C.	22	15
before you show someone respect, that person needs to earn it.................................	34	49
money is very important to you.................................	32	44
casino gambling should be allowed in all parts of the country.................................	29	42
even if a person has an incurable disease, a person should not be allowed to end his/her life......	27	17
the way things are these days, lying is sometimes necessary.................................	24	40
you favor the idea that homosexual adults should be able to get legally married..............	23	37

Source: Barna Research Group, Ltd., Ventura, CA;
1997 data, national samples.

TABLE 4.7
CHRISTIANS AND NON-CHRISTIANS NOTICEABLY DIFFER ON SOME ATTITUDES, OPINIONS AND VALUES

indicator	Christians	Non-Christians
abortion is morally wrong......................................	77%	52%
you, personally, find it annoying or bother some to hear profanity on radio programs.............	75	51
there are moral truths which are unchanging; they are not relative to the circumstances....	50	25
to get by in life these days, sometimes you have to bend the rules for your own benefit..........	35	57
whether or not it is acceptable to see pornographic videos or pictures is a matter of taste, not morality...	19	42

Source: Barna Research Group, Ltd., Ventura, CA; 1997 data, national samples.

TABLE 4.8
BELIEVERS AND NON-BELIEVERS BEHAVE ALMOST IDENTICALLY

indicator	Christians	Non-Christians
you consider yourself to be loving........................	99%	95%
you consider yourself to be happy........................	97	93
you have traditional moral standards....................	95	86
you consider yourself to be compassionate.......	94	95
went out of your way to encourage or complement someone within the past week for something excellent or special they had done................	86	77
donated money to a non-profit organization, other than a church, in the past month.............	47	48
it seems impossible to get ahead because of your financial debt......................................	33	39
drank an alcoholic beverage in the past month....	32	64
watched an R-rated movie in the past week..........	30	40
volunteered to help a non-profit organization, within the past week..	29	27
watched MTV within the past month....................	26	33
purchased a lottery ticket in the past week..........	23	27
gave money to a homeless/poor person you saw on the street within the past week.............	13	12
gambled or placed a bet in the past month..........	11	22
when a cashier gives you too much change, by mistake, you just let it go.................................	10	19

Source: Barna Research Group, Ltd., Ventura, CA; 1997 data, national samples.

What Does It Mean?

Clearly, impeccable historical foundations and the development of good intentions have not been enough to compel believers to lead a life that truly honors and serves Christ. We buy into the importance of worship without really knowing what it means or rarely engage in anything beyond rote behaviors. We are generally willing to share our faith, but huge numbers of believers never or rarely do so, and the content of our sharing is frightening. The biblical knowledge of born again believers is a combination of Scriptural substance and worldly wisdom blended into a distasteful theological mash. Believers have been incredibly blessed by God with material possessions, but we are loath to return the favor and invest in His priorities. We serve others when we must, but few believers have a love of serving people; our culture has seduced us into loving to be served, instead of committing ourselves to meeting the needs of others. We are good at relating to other believers, but not very good at having faith-based relationships in which our goal is to help each other mature in Christ. More often than not, our goal is to feel happy, comfortable and secure, and we surround ourselves with people who share a love of Christ and a willingness to affirm and appreciate us. Most disappointingly, we also find that the net outcome is a lifestyle that fails to demonstrate the practical realities of the Christian faith.

Is there room for improvement in the area of discipleship? You be the judge.

Footnotes
[1] Matthew 5:16
[2] Matthew 19:16-22
[3] Matthew 22:37-40
[4] Matthew 23:8-12
[5] Matthew 25:34-40
[6] Matthew 5 - 7
[7] John 2:17
[8] This chapter will not include an analysis of fellowship since I do not have

a good body of data on that component of our lives and ministry.

[9] The 13 items were: the Bible is totally accurate in all of its teachings; Satan is a symbol, not a living being, but a symbol of evil; a good person will earn a place in Heaven; Jesus committed sins; all religious faiths teach the same lessons; the Holy Spirit is a symbol of God's presence or power but is not a living entity; after he was crucified and died, Jesus Christ did not return to life physically; the Bible teaches that God helps those who help themselves; all people will experience the same outcome after death, regardless of their religious beliefs; some sins cannot be forgiven by God; angels exist and influence people's lives; the universe was originally created by God; the whole idea of sin is outdated. For further information on this research, see "American's Bible Knowledge Is In the Ballpark, But Often Off Base," The Barna Update, July 12, 2000, accessible on the Barna Research website (www.barna.org).

[10] For a more extensive discussion of moral truth and how the United States – and, especially, the Christian Church – caved in on absolute truth, see *Boiling Point*, George Barna and Mark Hatch, Regal Books (Ventura, CA), 2001.

[11] This principle was first communicated to us in Genesis 12:1-3, but constitutes a common thread of Jesus' teaching, as well.

[12] There are three types of averages: a mean, a median and a mode. The average referred to here is the median, which means that if we listed the total amounts donated by people during the year to their churches in order from least to most, the amount donated that falls exactly in the middle of that range would be the median. We use the median rather than the mean (which is derived by adding the total value of all contributions and dividing by the number of donors) to avoid distortions due to extreme amounts, at either the high or low ends of the scale.

[13] For additional information about giving patterns, read "Evangelicals Are the Most Generous Givers, But Fewer Than 10% of Born Again Christians Give 10% to Their Church," The Barna Update, April 5, 2000, accessible on the Barna Research website (www.barna.org).

[14] For more information about spiritual gifts, read Romans 12:6-8, 1 Corinthians 12:1-11, 1 Corinthians 12:28-31, Ephesians 4:11-13, and 1 Peter 4:10-11.

[15] The identification of a twenty-point difference as the cutoff for identifying truly significant attitudes, values, behaviors and beliefs is not as arbitrary as it may seem. It is based on the recognition that the average American has five people with whom he/she has a close, personal relationship. Consequently, a person is most likely to be influenced by the thoughts and deeds of those people. When one out of the five individuals in a person's circle of influencers (i.e., 20%) expresses a different viewpoint or demonstrates a behavior, the person is likely to notice that distinction. When two out of the five influencers (i.e., 40%) think or live differently, it will have a substantial impact on the person's personal choices. We originally found this to be pertinent among teenagers and have since seen that the same principle is at work in the lives of adults. Certainly, people

are influenced in many different ways and by different types of people. However, the most significant and lasting influences relate to personal relationships with trusted friends and family members.

CHAPTER 5

HOW WE GOT HERE – AND WHERE WE GO FROM HERE

In discussing the content of the previous chapter with a number of church leaders from around the country, there tended to be three common reactions to the state of the Church.

The first common reaction is to deny the facts. "I don't know who you talked to, but I know those figures can't be right. It's certainly not an accurate description of the people in my church. I know my people. They think and act differently than that," is a typical response from pastors. When I ask them how they know that their people are different from the national norms, the reply is also rather consistent: "I just know. I talk to them and they tell me things that are very different than what your numbers describe. Our church has been blessed with people who are more spiritually mature than most, partly because we do a good job of building them up in Christ." In other words, there is no objective measure of the alleged difference between their people and the Christian mass, but the typical leader believes that his people are different, based on assumptions, intuition and anecdotal evidence (i.e., personal stories).

The second common reaction is to feel discouraged. "Man, that's depressing. I almost feel like it's not worth continuing in ministry. After giving it our best shot, if that's the best we can produce, then why bother?" Again, there are assumptions underlying this viewpoint, e.g., we have done our best, that the current state of affairs is the best we can hope for, and that there are no alternative strategies to employ that might improve the product of our efforts.

The third common comeback is to appreciate and absorb the information because it clarifies the nature of the challenges and opportunities facing the Church. "Well, we certainly have our work cut out for us, don't we?" was the rhetorical question posed in response by one pastor I interviewed. "But it sure helps to know where we're falling short so that we can respond more appropriately to people's needs. Just look at the need and suffering out there! What a great time to be in ministry. If you can't make a difference in the midst of this situation, you probably can't make a difference anywhere!" In other words, rather than reject the findings as aberrant, these leaders accept the findings as insightful and motivating. They do not get hung up on the personal implications of the outcomes (e.g., "this means I'm a failure") or the magnitude of the challenge (e.g., "this is too big a job for us to tackle") but see the statistics as a progress report on an unfinished work (e.g., "it looks like we need to emphasize that aspect of ministry instead of this one").

As you reflect on the information described in the two earlier chapters, what was your gut reaction? If you're like many pastors and lay leaders, you might reject the findings outright. However, if you see the statistics as strategic wisdom that will make you a more effective servant of Christ, then you are probably going to be one of the church leaders who will bless Heaven, the Church and our society with irrefutable evidence that God is at work in the lives of His people. You are among the leaders God has raised up for a time such as this – a confusing, challenging, daunting era in which God's people have a unique capacity to restore our country to moral and spiritual sanity. If you remain focused and strategic in your ministry, you are likely to see dramatic results in people's lives as they struggle to grow in their faith.

How We Got to Where We Are

One hallmark of the most effective church leaders is not only that they refuse to accept defeat, but also that they strive to improve whatever they are doing. They love statistics and other objective evaluations of their situation because those indicators allow them to pinpoint what does and does not work, and to fine-tune their efforts and enhance their efficacy. They do not take personal offense at reports that suggest some of their efforts have failed to produce the desired results; they thrive on such reports because the information enables them to avoid wasting resources on unproductive activities.

As we evaluate the current condition of discipleship in the American Church – again, defined as activity that guides individuals to become spiritually mature zealots for Christ who then reproduce equally passionate and mature followers of Christ – we must take inventory and change those practices and perspectives that serve as obstacles to the desired outcome. What ideas and practices are responsible for causing the American Church to lose sight of the original, biblical goals of authentic worship, passionate commitment to spiritual development, sensitive yet strategic evangelism, consistent servanthood, loving and challenging relationships, and holistic stewardship?

Here are nine reasons that emerge from my research as to why we have struggled so mightily in the midst of an environment of unprecedented opportunity. In all likelihood, one or more of these barriers explains some of the difficulty you are facing in your ministry.

73

Reason #1:

Few churches or Christians have a clear and measurable definition of "spiritual success."

The old adage warns us "if you don't know where you're going, any road will take you there." That's an indictment of contemporary Christian discipleship. We have assumed that if a church provides consistent events, biblical information and appealing programs for people, and the people consume those offerings, then the users will grow. But we rarely stop to figure out in practical terms what God expects of us, or to assess how we measure up to those expectations, or to determine what we must do to improve our performance with respect to those desired outcomes.

Lacking a clear notion of what we're trying to become as believers, we often settle for something less than the biblical standard, and certainly less than what we are capable of becoming. Why not? If success is negotiable, why not include "comfortable and easily achievable growth" among the factors that make us successful?

How instructive it is to discover that when pressed to do so, not only have most Christians and most church leaders failed to specify what "spiritual success" means, but they do not feel compelled to work out a definition of such an endpoint or destination. The result has been that believers and churches embrace a cheap facsimile of spiritual success without remorse – or, in many cases, the realization that they have "dumbed down" Christianity.

Reason #2:

We have defined "discipleship" as head knowledge rather than complete transformation.

Talk to church leaders about their discipleship program and you usually hear about teaching events and programs. Sunday school, small groups, Christian education classes, seminary courses, study groups, reading groups, video curriculum, VBS – countless ways of communicating empirical information based on Scripture.

This is laudable and certainly needed. But filling people's heads with Bible verses and principles, alone, is inadequate. If you doubt that, please re-read the synoptic gospels and underline Jesus' words to the Pharisees and Sadducees during each encounter. The religious leaders of Jesus' time had memorized more Scripture and religious content than most of us can imagine. Yet, they were Jesus' models of how not to live. Why? Because they were all head and no heart. They knew the data, but ignored its application.

Perhaps more leaders than we know continue to follow the approach of Martin Luther, who disdained the book of James that is in the New Testament. Some accounts suggest that he wished it was not included in the canon of Scripture. But that letter to the leaders of the early Church is incredibly significant because it pounds away at one consistent message: faith that is not wholly integrated and consistently lived out is a charade. The issue is not that we must choose which element to esteem over the other – i.e., siding with either Bible knowledge or a righteous lifestyle – but that each must support the other.

The statistics in the preceding chapters underscore our need for both biblical knowledge and application of that knowledge in practical ways. Discipleship, defined as becoming spiritually mature in our imitation of Christ, demands that we give both the head and the heart sufficient opportunity to grow and to make a difference in our lives and in the world.

Reason #3:
We have chosen to teach people in random, rather than systematic, ways.

As we survey the practices of churches, we find that most churches are content to provide their people with biblical substance. The problem is not that the content itself is bad, but that the content is not provided in a purposeful, systematic manner. The result is that believers are exposed to good information without context and thus lose that information because they have no way of making sense of it within the bigger picture of faith and life. Consequently, we rate sermons on the basis of their value to what we're experiencing at the moment, or assess the usefulness of books and lessons in terms of how entertaining or erudite they are. Ultimately, believers become well-versed in knowing characters, stories, ideas and verses from the Bible, but remain clueless as to the importance of each.

Think of the way we teach people about Christianity as a massive game of "Connect the Dots." The problem is, in our version of the game, we do not put numbers next to the dots, rendering players incapable of connecting the dots in the fashion intended. All of the dots are provided and are pictured in exactly the right place, but without providing players with a sense of direction or the big picture, failure is inevitable.

Few churches intentionally guide their people through a strategic learning and developmental process that has been customized for the student. We push everyone through the same generic journey, expecting everyone to "get it" at the same time and in the same way, simultaneously developing into mature believers. It doesn't work that way. Until we assume a more strategic approach to delivering insights and outcomes within a viable mental and experiential framework, we will continue to be frustrated by the results of our well-intentioned but poorly conceptualized efforts to grow disciples.

Reason #4:
There is virtually no accountability for what we say, think, do or believe.

True growth demands accountability. However, few churches have systems by which they measure what is happening in the life of church adherents. Few believers have lined up a trustworthy and competent partner who will hold them accountable to specific and measurable goals. The result is that we operate on the basis of feelings, assumptions and hopes, rather than tangible, measurable realities.

Small groups may provide a viable content within which accountability may occur, but our studies show that such accountability is superficial and uncommon. We tend to be most focused upon evaluating people's knowledge; there are only limited attempts at holding people accountable to growth beyond information acquisition and retention.

Reason #5:
When it comes to discipleship, we promote programs rather than people.

How many churches have a dynamic database, or some other means of consistently and objectively tracking the spiritual development of individuals in the church? The answer is: very few. How many churches have created a successful mentoring or coaching program? Again, the answer is: very few. Why? Because a discipleship-oriented database implies both a commitment to staying in touch with people's growth and a desire to consistently improve the spiritual condition of the individuals in the church. Few churches have a life-changing mentoring or coaching program because such a process demands extensive knowledge of the qualities and capacities of the coach and the student, as well as the ability to wisely pair mentors with appropriate protégés. These are people-intensive processes. Most churches are not structured or emotionally geared to mastering such processes.

Even though churches claim that they are devoted to developing people, the most effective developmental procedures known to us today are generally ignored by those churches in favor of standardized programs, such as Sunday schools and small groups. Those programs are not bad; they have a useful place within a church. However, we should recognize that classes and groups, in addition to their positive developmental features, are often embraced as a way of organizing large groups of people into an orderly process that can be easily managed and controlled. If we were to be honest, we would have to admit that the absence of real measures of personal growth are a testimony to our concern about style more than substance, and our commitment to taking action more than having impact.

Personal development is not about maintaining control. It is about letting go to see what God, through His Holy Spirit, can do in the life of a believer who truly wants to mature in Christ. Just as Jesus accomplished the maturing of his followers through a personal relationship based upon creating a particular kind of person, so should we be wary of becoming too structured and programmatic.

Reason #6:
The primary method on which churches rely for spiritual development – small groups – typically fails to provide comprehensive spiritual nurture.

The problem is not the approach. Having small groups of people committed to helping each other grow can be an incredibly effective process. There is evidence of this in various churches across the nation and in the Bible. The reason why we don't see greater transformation through small groups is because we have not paid attention to the capabilities of the leaders and teachers in those groups, and the substance that gets shared in the group settings is often plagued by superficiality, misrepresentation or the absence of application. Too many resources are devoted to recruiting people for groups, and too few resources are spent preparing people to develop within them.

Reason #7:
Church leaders are not zealous about the spiritual development of people.

In our interviews with senior pastors from Protestant churches across the nation we discovered that these individuals give verbal support to the idea of spiritual growth, but often are not personally devoted to strenuously advocating spiritual transformation. This deficiency is witnessed in several ways. First, few congregants describe their pastor as a role model or as a zealot for Christ. While it is unhealthy to have the pastor placed on a pedestal as the paragon of Christianity, it is even more dangerous for the people not to have appropriate pride in the character and commitments of their spiritual leader. If nothing else, congregants ought to feel that they would be a better person if they were to follow the spiritual example set by their pastor. We find, however, that most believers have no clue what the spiritual life of their pastor is like and, therefore, have little impetus to emulate him/her.

Second, few pastors prioritize discipleship within their ministry. They may incorporate discipleship into the church's agenda, and ensure that some funding and warm bodies are allocated to the process, but they do not throw the full weight of their influence behind the significance of involvement in becoming spiritually mature. Promoting one ministry over another is one of the tough juggling acts that pastors perform. Every step along the way, advocates of one ministry or another – all of which are good, necessary, beneficial ministry ventures – are lobbying for the pastor's public support. But ultimately, that's what makes a great leader: the ability to juggle all of the possibilities successfully, while focusing the greatest quantity of resources on the most productive activities. To some extent the Christian church lacks real disciples because our spiritual leaders have inadequately prioritized that outcome.

Third, when pastors describe "success" for their church, attendance, revenue, programs and square footage constitute the practical dimensions of success. Surprisingly few pastors indicated that success relates to the spiritual quality of the lives of their congregants. More often, you hear about the quantity of people that participate in a group event or activity.

It is true that pastors do not have the professional weight or public standing they once did in America. However, among those within the church, the pastor is still a person of influence. One application of that influence relates to setting the ministry agenda – in terms of establishing the ministry priorities of the church and in directing people's attention to appropriate priorities in their own spiritual journey. When senior pastors downplay discipleship, the message comes through loud and clear: "it's helpful, but optional."

Reason #8:
We invest our resources in adults rather than children.

In all aspects of life people tend to do that which is most comfortable and natural for them. Perhaps that explains why we invest so much of the church's money on ministering to adults. If we were to objectively assess where we will get the greatest return on our investments, we would instead pour our resources into ministry to children. The work we have done in studying evangelism and discipleship has shown that once a person reaches the age of 12 or so, the chances of changing how they think and behave are limited. The chances of changing adults are very slim.

Does this insinuate that God cannot completely reform an individual, regardless of his/her age? No. Does it imply that I believe the Bible is wrong when it says that believers become regenerated beings after they encounter Christ? No. It is a simple recognition of human reality. Old habits are difficult to break. Established patterns of thought and behavior die hard. People can certainly change, no matter how young or old they are, but it is so much easier and it permeates the individual much more deeply when they are young. If we focus our energies on resuscitating adults, rather than children, we have more ground to cover because we have to undo much more than would be the case in working with children.

As Solomon once wrote, with great wisdom, "Train a child in the way he should go, and when he is old he will not depart from it."[1]

Reason #9:
We divert our best leaders to ministries other than discipleship.

A leader casts a compelling vision of a preferable future for people to embrace. It is that persuasive mental picture of a better self and better world that is used to motivate people to action. When you have an individual with good skills but little, if any, leadership ability, discipleship fails to get the motivation push that it requires. Congregants are busy. They are trying to make ends meet, keep the marriage and family together, maintain the house and yard, get ahead in their career, stay abreast of world events, stay physically fit, stay in touch with their friends and extended family, and invest their retirement funds wisely. In the midst of all of this, the church invites them to grow spiritually? "Why?," they ask. "I attend church pretty regularly, enroll the kids in Sunday school and VBS, put my hard-earned money in the offering basket each week, pray before meals and whenever else I get a spare moment, and try to read the Bible whenever the opportunity presents itself. How much more am I supposed to do for the church? It's just never enough!"

Without a true leader at the helm of the discipleship function, you almost cannot fault believers for missing the point. A leader would make the act of spiritual growth not seem like a chore, but a privilege; less of a command from God (though it is) and more of a glorious opportunity to join an elite group.

Leaders motivate, mobilize, direct and resource people to fulfill a vision. Too often, we present the options for personal growth and assume the people will latch on to the possibilities and benefits. When they don't climb on board, we shake our heads and rue their lack of commitment – without realizing that they are committed, but mostly to those things that fit within their vision of a meaningful life. The failure to instill competent leaders in the disciple-making process of the church has enabled them to completely misunderstand the choice they are making.

Where Do We Go From Here?

So where are trying to go with discipleship? What are the specific outcomes that we are striving to achieve, and what type of process will facilitate those elements? Here is my take on our objectives.

1. Passion

The true disciple of Jesus is someone who is completely sold out to Christianity. To determine whether you are really a disciple, the relevant question concerns your level of commitment: to what are you absolutely, fanatically devoted? Jesus did not minister, die and return to merely enlist fans. He gave everything He had to create a community of uncompromising zealots – raving, unequivocal, undeterable, no-holds-barred spiritual revolutionaries. He has no room for lukewarm followers.[2] He is not interested in those who have titles, prestige and self-sufficiency. He is searching for the broken, hopeless, helpless, spiritually dependent individuals who readily acknowledge that they cannot make headway without total and absolute dependence upon Jesus Christ. He is seeking the hearts of those who are willing to surrender everything for the blessed privilege of suffering for Him, just as He suffered for us. He wants people who are dedicated to getting beyond the offer of mere salvation to those willing to do what it takes to complete personal transformation. Discipleship is a lifelong calling that demands every resource we will ever muster. Discipleship is about passion to reach our full potential in Christ.

2. Maturity in the fundamentals of ministry

There are a small number of ministry components to which we must be dedicated. Those include worship, evangelism, discipleship, servanthood, stewardship, and fellowship. In other words, we are to dive into a process that will facilitate personal spiritual formation, molding us into the likeness of our ultimate role model, Jesus Christ. Our discipleship, or personal spiritual growth, efforts ought to be designed to develop us in these six primary areas. There are many related activities, of course – prayer, confession, etc. – but our energies should be geared to strategically improving ourselves in these core dimensions.

3. A biblical worldview

If you are to act like a Christian, you must think like a Christian. To think like a Christian, you need to be fully immersed in the knowledge of your faith and the application of its principles in godly practices. Because every thought, word and deed has consequences, every choice we make must be carefully considered. The only way to truly ensure that we optimize our opportunities in life and represent Christ well in every episode in our lives is to respond to reality on the basis of a Bible-based worldview. In other words, we must filter every choice through a mind and heart that are so saturated with God's perspectives that our choices reflect His choices. Our fallen nature prevents us from flawlessly representing the ways of God, but the more we own His truths and principles, the better we will be at living a truly Christian life.

4. Standards and accountability that foster spiritual growth

Human nature distorts our perspective. Rather than set our sights on the ultimate prize and sacrifice whatever it takes to reach that goal, we usually slither down the path of least resistance and get by as simply as possible. Christian discipleship deems such behavior a failure. We serve a perfect, holy, omnipotent God who yearns for us to imitate His Son. To settle for anything less than our absolute best is disrespectful and indefensible.

However, because we live in a world that accepts second best and half-hearted efforts, we often set our sights lower than we should. Only through adhering to a tireless process of accountability, in which we are motivated and pushed to reach high standards, will we rise to the heights God intends for us to reach. Left to our own devices, we can fool ourselves into believing that we have done better than before, perhaps even the best we can hope to achieve, when in fact we have barely nudged ourselves forward. Reliance upon a community of loving and supportive but high-minded peers in Christ is necessary if we are to make true progress in our spiritual development.

What's Barna Been Smokin'?

Not too long ago I had a conversation with the pastor of a rather large church. We have become friendly enough that we can shred each other's best ideas and analyses without offending or emotionally crippling each other. I ran these ideas past him.

He laughed. He caught his breath, stared at me seriously for a few moments, then burst out laughing some more. Once he regained his composure, he drilled into me. "Barna, what have you been smokin', man? Pass me that pipe, brother, 'cause I want to leave reality to experience your plane of existence. Are you nuts? I dare you to name me one church – *just one* – anywhere in this entire nation of ours that does what you just described. You armchair theoreticians make me nauseous. You're probably going to write this wacko idea in a book and make thousands of pastors suffer guilt meltdown because they haven't reached this mythical nirvana that you're proposing as a standard. Go ahead, name me one church that does these things."

Our debate raised some wonderful – and, for me, deeply disturbing – questions. Is it expecting too much to see such deep, life transformation occur in 21st century America? In a world where people are ruled by their calendars, and the rule of the calendar is "no more – all full," is it reasonable to expect people to prioritize spiritual growth? In an age where the pace of life sucks the energy out of us, is it feasible that people could be passionate about something as seemingly intangible as faith? In a world in which relativism and tolerance reign, are we just fooling ourselves to imagine that Christians might be willing to depart from the norm and voluntarily submit themselves to honest scrutiny and evaluation by peers who will judge them, in love? In a nation where we're fortunate to get people to remember that the Old Testament precedes the New Testament in the Bible, is it within the boundaries of possibility that Christians can adopt a biblical worldview that does truly change the way they think and behave, every moment of every day? Is there a church anywhere that really accomplishes these things?

My friend's laughter rang in my ears for months. In fact, for the first few months I seriously questioned whether to continue our research on this topic. Several hours of harassment from him regarding the practical obstacles of creating a community of faith such as I had described had taken their toll on my mind. Truthfully, it was nothing more noble than a desire to finish what I had started and to get some benefit from the huge research investment our company had already made that compelled me to complete the research project regarding discipleship. I decided that we would carry out the final step in the 2-year process, that of beating the bushes throughout America to locate and then study churches that do great discipleship ministry.

To God's glory – and my relief – now it's my turn to laugh. The next two chapters of this book will describe for you the inner workings of two dozen churches we studied in depth that are doing the very things detailed in the preceding section of this chapter. Chapter six will discuss many of the common characteristics that these churches possess and that you, too, can embrace in your ministry, regardless of its size, theological leanings, or target audience. Chapter seven will give you five specific models through which these stellar churches accomplish such audacious ends. The results achieved by these churches are what business gurus James Collins would call a BHAG (i.e., a big, hairy, audacious goal) or Tom Peters would label "WOW!" (as in "this is *incredible* – where do I sign up?").[3] If you felt weighed down by the depressing statistics and descriptions in chapter four, then don't give up yet. Turn the page, for the next two chapters should lift your spirits and stimulate your mind and heart to devote yourself to developing a discipleship process that wins hearty shouts of "I *love* Jesus! I *love* this church! I *love* being a Christian!" from your congregants.

We have made mistakes in the church. We have failed our Lord and we have failed His people. It's time to get it right. Let's learn from our pioneering colleagues who have blazed the trail for us.

Footnotes

[1] Proverbs 22:6

[2] Revelation 3:15-16

[3] Reading the work of these men would be helpful, even though their focus is upon business and profitability. Take a look at *Built to Last*, James Collins and Jerry Porras, Harper Business, New York, 1994; and *The Tom Peters Seminar*, Tom Peters, Vintage Books, New York, 1994.

CHAPTER 6

HIGHLY EFFECTIVE
DISCIPLESHIP WITHIN
CHURCHES

Let me tell you how various churches across the nation are producing true disciples of Jesus Christ. We had the privilege of studying more than a dozen churches, in depth, to determine what makes these ministries so effective. We discovered that they share some common perspectives and practices regarding discipleship. We also found that there seem to be five distinctive models by which these churches facilitate genuine followers of Christ. In this chapter I will describe the perspectives and practices shared by the churches that are producing great disciples. In the next chapter I will distill the core components of the five models.

What makes me claim that these churches are doing a great job? First, they are regarded by other ministry professionals as experts in this arena of ministry. In most cases, it was the recommendations of people who have experience in working with or studying hundreds of churches that directed our attention toward these places. But we know very well that appearances can be deceiving, and that outsiders sometimes misjudge the true state of affairs at a church. So our second requirement was that we conduct extensive interviews with the leaders of these churches, and ask probing questions to get at what really happens. Interestingly, more than half of the churches that were originally recommended to us as being highly effective at disciple-making were eliminated once we completed this level of interviews. Finally, in most cases one or more of our staff spent some time, typically incognito, experiencing and observing what actually happens at the church. The result is a rather well-rounded examination of the spiritual development process at these churches.

The size of the churches we studied most closely ranged from 150 up to about 4500 adults attending the church on a typical weekend. The churches in our sample that have the fewest people – i.e., those attracting 150 or so adults – are probably not of that size anymore. By the time you read this chapter they will probably have eclipsed the 200 mark and will be inexorably headed toward 300 and beyond. I had hoped to have a wealth of great discipling churches in the 100 to 400-adult range, but quickly learned that a church engaged in effective discipleship is a church that will grow steadily and solidly. Why? Because people love to be cared for; a church that emphasizes genuine spiritual care and facilitates real spiritual growth will be a magnet. This is like a parent-child relationship. A loving parent disciplines the child. The child overtly complains about the discipline but covertly cherishes that shaping influence, recognizing that it reflects the parent's love for the child and is in the best long-term interests of the child. Christians are the same way. We may complain about all the effort it takes to become a true disciple, but the more people sense that the church's regimen is not just busy work but is truly developmental, the more committed they become to the process – and the more other people are attracted to that church.

By the way, the highly effective disciple-making churches we studied come from a wide variety of theological positions (both sides of the Calvinist-Wesleyan divide), geographic locations (all four regions), and ages (churches ranging from seven years old to more than 150 years old).

Baseline Definitions

When we asked the church leaders to describe what discipleship means to them, no two churches gave exactly the same definition. However, we found that there were nine elements that their definitions had in common.

- *Passion*: each church understood that discipleship without passion was merely organizational programming. Several churches arrived at the importance of passion by having spent years struggling to develop a process that worked – and learning that until the people are passionate about becoming Christ-like, no amount of great teaching or cutting edge techniques will get you where you need to go.

- *Depth*: the ultimate objective is to enable people to plumb the depths of the Christian faith and truly "own" it. Extensive knowledge about Christianity is insufficient. Extensive ministry activity is, in itself, insufficient. Personal growth without reproduction is indefensible. These churches are committed to fostering the development of completely-Christian believers.

- *Maturity*: the end product is for the person to reach his/her highest earthly potential in Christ. Complete development is the end; total personal commitment to becoming spiritually mature is one of the early indicators of success in the process.

- *Practice*: the emphasis is not upon knowing what it means to be a mature Christian, or knowing how to become spiritually mature. It is based upon being spiritually mature – that is, knowing, doing and being all that Christ has called us to be.

- *Process*: discipleship is not a destination but a journey. We will never achieve complete spiritual maturity this side of Heaven. We may, however, enjoy the journey and grow as we pursue spiritual completeness.

- *Interactive*: discipleship must be done in community, rather than in isolation. Other people provide a level of objectivity, accountability, creativity and encouragement that we cannot, by ourselves, muster.

- *Multi-faceted*: the process incorporates a variety of thrusts toward building us up in Christ. Just as the church is to encompass several specific ministry thrusts, so should each disciple grow in various areas of spiritual maturity.

- *Lifelong*: it is not possible to complete the process of becoming spiritually mature. Therefore, we must be involved in discipleship for the long-term, engaged in a permanent process of shaping and being shaped, of struggling and mastering.

- *Christ-like*: the model of our efforts is Jesus Christ. When we lose a sense of how we're doing, what we're striving to achieve or what else we must incorporate into the process, the definitive marker is the Lord Himself. All other models are mere imitations; our true point of comparison is Jesus.

Each church we studied had a different emphasis in its definition of discipleship, but these elements tended to be present, to some degree, in their description of their process.

Success in Discipleship

Again, each church had its own way of communicating what "successful discipleship" means, in practical terms, but the nature of their descriptions was similar. Some churches discussed specific ministry outcomes related to worship, evangelism, service, and knowledge. Other churches talked about more general measures, such as personal empowerment, consistent growth, exploitation of their gifts, or a deepening relationship with Jesus Christ. A few churches identified Bible passages, such as Galatians 5:22-24 (fruit of the Spirit) or 1 Timothy 3 (character qualities) as the substance they refer to when assessing their progress.

Assessment of Development

When it comes to evaluating how well people are doing in their effort to emulate Christ, the truly effective churches go beyond the collection and recitation of affirming anecdotes. Each of these churches had specific tools that they used – most of them developed in-house – that provide a sense of what is happening spiritually in people's lives. These tools included knowledge measurements, behavioral assessments, gift inventories, attitudinal and behavioral surveys, goal statements and measurements, and the like. No church argued that those inventories provide a completely accurate picture of reality; instead, they viewed their tools as flawed, but objective and relatively consistent instruments that aided in determining whether progress was being made from year to year. The purpose of the tools was not to claim with certainty that a specific percentage of the congregation knew a given principle or behaved in a particular way, but to indicate that compared to a year ago, or in relation to goals that had been set by congregants, the church was at a given level of achievement.

I was impressed by the sensitivity the church's leaders displayed regarding the frailty of their instruments – and their commitment to the necessity of using some tangible, objective yardsticks of progress. "If all I have to rely on is my people's say-so about their growth, I'm in trouble. It's just human nature for us to overestimate our own progress," explained one of the pastors. "I need something that takes the measurement process out of my hands, so I'm not the bad guy, but that gives me something I can ask them about, so that I can hold them accountable to something we've both agreed upon."

The measures used by the church were not limited to the personal growth assessments carried out by individuals. Most churches used other general measures of the well-being and health of the church in addition to the cumulative state of the individual measures. General factors such as the numbers of volunteers, how easy or difficult it is to recruit people to assume ministry responsibilities (e.g., Sunday school teachers, feeding the homeless, maintaining the church buildings), the number of people who turn in a personal growth plan, the number of visitors attending the church, the number of divorces among congregants, the number of serious friendships developing among congregants, people's desire to go overseas on short-term missions projects, and even the level of sophistication observed by small group overseers were examples of the more "touchy-feely" measures considered by church leaders.

One outcome that was mentioned by only one pastor, but that seems critical for success, was experiencing the joy of growth. "Are they enjoying it? Because at the end of the day, if they say 'Man, this last year was like boot camp, I'm sure glad it's over with,' then they're never going to do it again. If that happens, then we really haven't achieved our end because our aim, as the Westminster Catechism would teach it, is to glorify God and to enjoy Him." This pastor serves a church that is constantly refining its process, but has exploded with growth in the southeast over the last twenty years. "[We're looking for people to say] 'I am enjoying and delighting in doing. I love this discipleship stuff. I love getting to know more about Christ, about who He is, and I'm going to go out and get other people to come into my group next year because it is so good. I loved doing this and I want more people to do it with me next year.' That would probably be the ultimate mark of success for us."

There are, of course, a variety of personal indicators of growth that the church encourages people to rely upon. These included evaluations of how they are doing in reaching their pre-determined spiritual goals; discussions with family and small group members regarding progress; filling out church-developed or standardized assessment tools; having regular advisory sessions with more mature Christians to discuss growth patterns and experiences; encouraging people to journal, and to read previous journal entries to sense progress or barriers; challenging people to identify ways in which they applied the lessons from recent sermons; and reflective prayer, seeking direct revelation from God as to what is and is not working in the developmental efforts.

As a general guideline, we discovered that the typical disciple devotes an average of four to six hours per week to spiritual development efforts beyond attending the worship service.

Inclusiveness

There were some theological issues related to whom these churches would invest their resources in: some churches invite everyone to get involved in a full-fledged discipleship program, whether they are saved or not, while others make discipleship one of the benefits available to believers. The general consensus, however, was that somewhere in the neighborhood of 50% to 65% of the congregation's adults were presently involved in a serious process of spiritual development. The low end of the scale was 40%; the upper end was 80%.

These figures were based upon some fairly demanding measures of consistent commitment to growth. Worthy of note is the fact that these pastors had a very solid understanding of the proportion of adults who were involved in a discipleship process. When we quizzed them as to the basis of the figures they were using, each of them had solid, substantive reasons for the participation figures they were suggesting. The implication: they care about the discipleship commitment of their people, they monitor it closely, and they respond when the numbers suggest a waffling of dedication to spiritual advancement.

Another key to the process is beginning it before a person reaches adulthood; not one of the highly effective churches waits until a person is 18 or 21 to begin an intensive and intentional discipling process. Each church had its own starting point and reasons for why they start discipling people at that age. One church begins kids in pre-school with a regimen of principles (based on stories) and practices (group activities) that fits within a long-term plan for the spiritual shaping of individuals. We encountered at least one highly effective disciple-making church that initiates their discipleship process in any given grade level, ranging from first grade through ninth grade. Most impressive was the fact that each church had a reason – usually based on developmental psychology or other behavioral and educational research – as to why they begin the process at that particular age or grade level. Clearly, this is a matter that has received much thought and testing with the goal of maximizing the potential for growing genuine followers of Christ.

Coordinating the Activities

About half of these churches coordinate all of the church teaching and activity across age groups. In other words, the substantive focus of the church during any given week is coordinated around a particular principle, Bible passage or developmental theme. The coordination includes the sermon topic; Sunday school lessons; small groups lessons; church prayer meetings; and special community service options.

About one-quarter of the churches coordinate these elements within specific age groupings: for instance, all adult activities, and all children's activities will be content coordinated, although the content might not be the same in the adult program as in the children's program. The most common reason for this separation is the difficulty of keeping young people and older people moving forward at the same pace and emphasizing the same topics while maintaining church-wide enthusiasm for the process and its substance.

The Driving Force

In the highly effective disciple-making churches, the senior pastor was acknowledged to be the catalyst behind the commitment to spiritual growth. In most cases the day to day management of the process has been handed over to someone on staff or to an elder or other lay leader. However, most of the people we interviewed suggested that it is the passion of the senior pastor to the process that prevents the church from becoming lazy in this dimension of ministry.

The role of the pastor is usually one of providing vision for the program, motivation to the congregation, and ensuring that the resources are available to carry on the ministry. In other words, these pastors are truly operating as leaders – individuals who motivate people on the basis of a vision for discipleship, mobilizing people to engage in purposeful participation, providing general direction for the process, and providing the resources necessary to get the job done. Often, after delivering such leadership, the process runs its course under the supervision of skilled individuals who have bought the vision and become its advocates.

For context, we also interviewed pastors and leaders in many churches that are not doing well in discipleship. In almost every case, we learned that either the senior pastor is silent about discipleship, or merely gives lip service to its importance.

Elements in the Process

Among the highly effective churches, no two of them had exactly the same process in place. Among the common elements included were small groups; sermons tied to practical applications and a long-term plan of specific content to be delivered; new believer classes; leadership training programs; one to one mentoring; Bible memorization; Sunday school classes (especially the progressive, 101, 201, 301 variety); community service ministry groups; online curriculum; "mini-church" events; 2-year or 3-year classes on worldview foundations; daily Bible reading programs; a wide variety of ministry events; book discussion groups; life plan development; gift assessment and activation; and a large-group discipleship training process (i.e., a typical classroom instruction approach). (In the next chapter I will describe four rather well-developed models of how some of these elements might be blended together to create a powerful developmental process.)

It may be helpful to identify some of the developmental approaches that typically failed to produce the desired results. The flawed approaches included the following:

✗ trying to produce disciples without first having a clear, crisp and compelling definition of discipleship

✗ using discipleship curriculum developed by any of the large, highly-regarded churches

✗ doing discipleship activities without having a well-conceived, long-term discipleship strategy as the foundation for decision-making, resource allocation and ministry implementation

✗ using small groups as a forum for evangelism

✗ emphasizing biblical knowledge without a complimentary emphasis upon behavioral change.

In relation to specific resources, few existing tools proved to be very helpful to their efforts. While most of the materials these churches use were developed in-house, here are a few tools that some churches said had been useful additions to the materials and resources they had created.

✓ topical small group materials from a range of organizations and individuals (including Willow Creek, Serendipity, the Navigators, Kay Arthur, and Beth Moore)

✓ Rick Warren's book, *The Purpose-Driven Church*

✓ *Experiencing God*, by Henry Blackaby and Claude King

✓ daily devotional guides, especially when tied to other church-driven content

Among the available tools that were generally panned by these churches were standardized curriculum (disparaged by pastors as being too generic, too rigid, too linear, and too boring); videos (deemed potentially useful as discussion starters, but rather useless as a teaching supplement if they run more than 10 minutes); and standardized evangelism programs (too hokey, often focused on techniques rather than hearts).

About half of these churches use events successfully to motivate people to engage in discipleship or to further their development. About one-quarter has tried various events and has abandoned the practice after finding them to be fruitless. The remaining one-quarter has avoided events altogether based on a philosophical concern about reliance upon them. Among the events that have produced good results for the event-using churches were Vacation Bible School (VBS), community service outreaches, small-group introductory events; relationship-building activities; and family development adventures.

Perhaps the most popular tactic is to motivate people to join a small group within which to experience a more personal discipling environment. Although a handful of these churches tried small groups and disbanded them because they did not generate the desired results, most others consider these small, home-based, church-directed aggregations to be the cornerstone of their development process. However, most of these churches also acknowledge that unless there is ample facilitator training, a tight accountability process, strong relational connections developed, and a purposeful selection of material to cover within the groups, the groups will fail to produce disciples. Most of these churches establish groups that run for an academic year (i.e., September through June), are disbanded for the summer, then may re-form during the next academic year.

Sunday school classes are most commonly used by Southern Baptist churches in their discipleship efforts. Relatively few of the other highly effective disciple-making churches we studied rely upon Sunday school classes for adults; most of them do use such classes for the shaping of young people. A popular adult alternative is the "Adult Bible Fellowship," (ABF) used in several of the effective congregations. An ABF is essentially a content-heavy, mid-sized teaching experience in which a collection of small groups, comprising anywhere between 30 to 80 people, meets together each Sunday morning, either before or after the worship service. The primary purpose of the ABF is to give people high quality Bible teaching; each ABF is taught the same material on any given week, and the content is related to that week's sermon. This frees small groups to discuss applications, to implement accountability and to develop more intimate relationships. The ABF approach typically is used in tandem with small groups, serving as a segue from the large group worship-driven experience in the sanctuary to the intimacy and lifestyle transformation orientation of the small group.

Many churches also rely upon topical Christian education classes designed to fill in the gaps of people's spiritual understanding, or to polish skills they want to hone, or to introduce them to matters that they think might be of value or interest but will not be touched upon in their other discipleship venues. The topics covered in such classes run the gamut, from learning Greek and Hebrew to discovering how to study the Bible or how to make a friend among non-Christians. Few of the churches we studied consider these classes to be integral elements of the disciple-making process; the classes are more of a community service than a core component. In a few churches, such topical courses were offered as the summertime replacement for the small groups that do not meet during July and August.

Most of the highly effective disciple-making churches integrate mentoring or coaching into their process. The ways in which this happens varies tremendously. Some churches raise up future leaders and teachers by having them serve as apprentices to church staff. Other congregations have more traditional one-to-one matches, with one individual serving as the discipler and the other as the disciple. Some churches modify that approach and use an "accountability partner" model – both people on equal footing, meeting regularly to talk, to pray and to challenge each other spiritually. Several congregations used a trickle-down model: staff person mentors a half dozen lay people, each of those people mentor from two to six other congregants, and each of those people does the same.

Each of the churches we studied is sold on the value of mentoring; only one church had such a bad experience that they have abandoned the practice. The toughest jobs, we discovered, are training people to be effective mentors (not everyone is good at this, of course); knowing how to integrate someone into the flow when they are not a skilled mentor (and do not possess much mentoring potential); keeping people's time commitment up to snuff; and preventing the mentoring process from becoming strictly a fellowship effort.

Few churches use the Internet for anything more than an information dumping ground; we did not discover any innovative or productive uses of the Net for discipleship. A handful of churches try to shake up the predictability of the process by using a tape, book or other outside resource as a focal point for interaction among people. (This is done in different ways: encouraging people to get the resource and engage someone in conversation on it; inviting people to a church-wide event, held monthly or quarterly, to interact on that resource; and so forth.)

Personal Encouragement

Every church struggles with the challenge of motivating people to get involved and to stay involved in discipleship. Even people who enjoy the process and realize how beneficial it is go through periods of time when the pressures of life obscure the sense of value and fulfillment that closeness to God brings. How do churches handle these challenges?

One of the most common approaches was to empower people to challenge each other once they have developed trust-based relationships. Small groups have been good vehicles for facilitating this outcome. Pastors noted that when their peers are growing, people feel unstated pressure to stay focused on growth. There is a tremendous uplifting presence experienced in the company of other believers who are also striving to grow. Being encouraged and guided by one's spiritual family is a powerful catalyst to perpetual effort, if not to constant development.

Most highly effective ministries also encourage people to put reasonable pressure on themselves to grow by having them identify their personal growth goals for the year. The beauty of this approach is that the individual cannot reject the goals as having been imposed by an organization or by someone else; they designated the desired outcomes of their own free will and cannot blame anyone else for the challenges those goals present. In addition to specifying the outcomes they hope to achieve, and signing a commitment form in relation to those objectives, a regular evaluation of progress that has been made – for instance, a quarterly reassessment session – keeps people on-track.

Many of these churches incorporate testimonies and other "success stories" into the church's regular events (e.g., worship services). One purpose of these interviews and monologues is to encourage those exposed to the success of peers to sustain their commitment to growth. "Sometimes people just get tired or feel like they can't climb the hill," related one pastor who has a 5-minute slot in the weekly worship service for a personal testimony about spiritual growth by a teenager or adult from the congregation. "But when they see Betty Jane or Max stand up there – they know these people – and hear what God is doing through them, largely due to perseverance, then everyone re-thinks their own struggles and realizes, 'Man, if Max can do that, I bet I can, too.' We're not making heroes out of these people, but just showing what happens when you stick to it and allow God to change you, no matter how inferior or incapable you feel."

The Indispensable Resources

Various resources were listed as "indispensable" for successful discipleship by the leaders of these churches. High quality, well-trained leaders was the most frequently mentioned need. Passion for Christ and to live like Him was a close second – and instigating such a desire is, also, largely a leadership function. Vision and clarity of purpose were deemed necessary by most of these churches, along with a church-wide commitment to Scripture, opportunities to build meaningful relationships that lead to accountability, and ample opportunities to use one's gifts.

It may be equally instructive to note the resources that were not listed, even once, by these two dozen churches. Among them were: money, staff, facilities, and curriculum. In other words, all of the resources typically required to run a successful program were not thought of as relevant in regard to an effective discipleship ministry. It is a lay-driven endeavor that demands a culture of commitment, responsibility and growth. Those components require leadership, desire and perseverance more than a bank account, a central meeting place and experts directing people's energies.

Advice to Others

The pastors of the highly effective disciple-making churches are well aware that the level of productivity they have fostered at their churches is not the norm. Many of them have labored at other churches, or even at their present church, under circumstances that are similar to that of most churches. They comprehend the magnitude and the nature of the challenge facing most churches. What would they recommend to other churches that are interested in upgrading their level of discipleship? Here is a summary of the advice they gave.

- Recognize that disciple-making is a process, not a program. It is about building people, not creating methods and systems. More important than anything else is to develop a church-wide culture that esteems becoming a disciple.

- The process will not occur without leadership from the senior pastor. Motivating widespread and diligent participation cannot be delegated to a staff person or lay leader. They may be able to move the process forward, but they will not get the process off the ground: the weight of the senior leader's commitment to personal spiritual growth is required to initiate the process.

- The church's ministry focus must be streamlined to prioritize and support discipleship. That includes establishing genuine spiritual growth as a core element of the church's mission; providing a clear definition of discipleship; instituting a compelling motivation for involvement; eliminating programs and ministries that divert people's attention and the church's resources; determining the practical realities of facilitating spiritual transformation; and creating dynamic means of enabling people to grow.

- The process is not likely to succeed unless there is a simple but intelligent plan for growth. That plan must include measurable objectives and be consistently promoted and worked through by the church's leaders.

- The process will not generate true disciples unless it has a designated supervisor to facilitate progress, to foster creative problem-solving and development, and to strive for reasonable outcomes. Setting out to realize growth goals that are too substantial, too sophisticated and that must happen too quickly, will produce discouragement and failure. Start small, experimenting with your process to see what works best within your culture. Let those disciples then become not only your "trophies," but also your advocates of effective disciple-making. Establish reasonable outcomes that are challenging but achievable. Becoming a disciple is a lifelong process; transitioning a church from developing observers into disciples will not be accomplished overnight.

- In creating a process that works, adapt lessons learned by other effective disciple-making churches to your own

102

unique ministry context. There's no sense in re-creating the wheel, but there's also no wisdom in simply copying what another church has done in a different ministry context. Use the principles that they have learned to further your own efforts.

- Be prepared for burnout and complacency to set in after two or three years of involvement in an intensive process. This tendency to depart from the process can be diffused by building a ministry environment in which almost everyone is involved in discipleship; in which leaders do not accept any excuses for a desire to depart from the process; and where the culture demands consistent participation in spiritual growth activities.

- Carefully balance the competing interests of flexibility and structure. People need to be motivated and organized, but they also need to be given some room to develop procedures that reflect who they are, where they are going, and what will generate the best results. Achieving and maintaining that balance necessitates strong, competent leadership. If the leaders are going to err in fostering that balance, they should err on the side of demanding biblical substance (rather than other emphases) and clear, unified direction (rather than well-intentioned but disjointed progress).

No Easy Task

Let me close this chapter with two cautions. First, you may read the elements contained in this chapter and nod your head approvingly, as if you've heard this all before (you probably have) and as if it's no big deal. That's where you're wrong. This is a big deal. For these churches to have not only gathered the knowledge of what it takes to disciple people, but to have changed their church's heartbeat in order to facilitate life transformation in the prescribed ways, is breathtaking. Many pastors and church leaders have the knowledge. Very few are implementing that information in ways that produce true disciples. Do not minimize the significance of the connection between knowledge and practice. What these churches are doing is profound.

Second, realize that, like you, these churches face daily barriers to success in disciple-making. The dominant obstacles they identified will be familiar to you: people's time pressures, the lack of motivation to become Christ-like, cultural and demographic differences that preclude one-size-fits-all programs from working; the tendency to give up midway through a taxing process; internal competition with other church activities and programs; negative preconceived notions about "discipleship;" reliance upon strict linear learning patterns; the lack of role models; narcissism, hardened hearts and cheap grace; the church's program orientation; and people's belief that such an effort will produce in significant results. Do these roadblocks sound familiar?

The leaders of these churches remind us that we are ministering to a different group of people, who have different needs, in a different culture than was true even ten years ago. People are used to changing their plans on a moment's notice, so getting long-term, inflexible commitments from disciples is tougher. We are drenched in information, so our information absorption and analysis skills have changed significantly. Technology, performance pressures and lifestyle shifts have isolated individuals, causing them to be more open to relationships developed through church connections. Having been burned time after time, people are now more suspicious of offers of a quick fix, and they also demand persuasive demonstrations of relevance prior to their making a commitment to anything. We have less of a knowledge base to build upon, and must provide depth within the context of experience.

The experiences of these churches remind us not to fall prey to comfortable assumptions: e.g., all it takes is good preaching to produce true disciples, using the best curriculum money can buy will grow people spiritually, hiring competent staff is sufficient to move the process along, placing a large proportion of people in small groups generates true disciples. These assumptions are inaccurate more often than they prove to be true. Having a realistic, appropriate view of people's needs and of the impact of the process, as well as an accurate assessment of what types of change are actually happening, are important elements to design into the process you employ.

Keep your eyes on the goal: we are dedicated to producing genuine followers of Jesus. That demands people developing a biblical worldview and a compassionate heart. The highly effective disciple-making churches dwell on how they can direct peoples' minds, hearts and energy toward being devoted to living a transformed life. They are not perfect churches and they do not have perfect disciples. But they're getting closer to those outcomes, day by day, by virtue of their clearly articulated, single-minded devotion to such outcomes.

CHAPTER 7

FIVE MODELS OF DISCIPLESHIP

In studying the churches that are developing passionate, mature followers of Jesus Christ, I noticed that there were five particular approaches that facilitate these outcomes. The approaches have many similarities but also some unique twists that qualify them as different models. In this chapter I will give you a brief overview of each model.

For the sake of distinguishing these models in the course of this discussion, I will use the following names for these models:

1. the **Competencies model**,
used at Pantego Bible Church (PBC)[1]

2. the **Missional model**,
practiced at Fellowship Bible Church of Little Rock (FBCLR)[2]

3. the **Neighborhood model**,
developed by Perimeter Church[3]

4. the **Worldview model**,
as practiced at Fellowship Bible Church North (FBCN)[4]

5. and the **Lecture-Lab model**,
developed by North Coast Church (NCC).[5]

All five models emphasize enabling people to think and act like Christians. All five models focus on character development, thinking and decision-making, and building affirming relationships. How each model accomplishes these tasks is where the differences lie. Our observation is that all five models have great potential to produce zealots for Christ – people who "get it" and who live it. Let's take a brief look at each approach.[6]

1. The Competencies Model

This model is a highly integrated approach to discipleship that stands out for its emphasis upon personal assessment and integration with all aspects of the ministry. The model is based on the Great Commandment and the Great Commission, broken into 30 specific foci: 10 core belief dimensions, 10 core practices, and 10 core virtues. The process considers these 30 dimensions in light of one's relationship with God and with other people. Specifically, here are the competencies:

Beliefs	Practices	Virtues
the Trinity	worship	joy
salvation by grace	prayer	peace
authority of the Bible	single-mindedness	faithfulness
personal God	Bible study	self-control
identity in Christ	total commitment	humility
church	biblical community	love
humanity	give away your time	patience
compassion	give away your money	integrity
eternity	give away your faith	kindness
stewardship	give away your life	gentleness

This model requires the substantive integration of everything the church does. The worship services provide inspiration to become a disciple, and the sermons are built around the 30 core competencies. People receive their primary theological instruction in a modified

Sunday school/Adult Bible Fellowship process in which several small groups from a particular geographic area are combined into a learning community. These groups have a trained lay pastor and encompass 30 to 50 people from a common geographic area. That group meets every Sunday morning at the church campus to discuss the sermon topic.

Individuals then become active in ministry by belonging to a small group of 10 to 12 people in number, based on geographic and life stage similarities, such as young married couples or empy nesters. The dominant function of that group is to be a biblical community – putting into practice the information and principles learned in the larger group events. Small groups have a trained leader and are held accountable for specific outcomes related to service, evangelism, learning and care-giving.

Each individual is expected to not only engage with the congregation through the worship service, the mid-sized teaching community and the small group, but to commit to personal development in specific competencies. The areas of competence that most need attention are identified through the annual use of a personal spiritual evaluation tool, the Christian Life Profile, which contains 120 questions (four items per competency). In addition to self-assessment, three other individuals in the small group complete an abbreviated version of the assessment related to the person, evaluating his/her virtues. The results give the individual a sense of where his/her spiritual formation may be most lacking. The small group then provides prayer support and encouragement throughout the year as the person strives to improve in that area.

The results of a person's assessment are not compared to those of other individuals, but become self-regulating indicators of personal strengths and weaknesses. Over the course of time, as the individual completes several of these assessments, the results become a personal trend line marking relative growth or stagnation. The Profile is a tool to help the individual intentionally focus on his/her spiritual condition and to facilitate an appropriate domain of spiritual formation emphasis.

109

In addition, the church offers a range of topical classes that deal with the competencies. Nobody is required to attend these classes, but individuals who wish to develop in specific areas and who need more focused instruction and guidance than is available in the other groups, may take advantage of these classes.

Thus, every week it is possible for an individual to have five different church-based experiences that focus on the competencies. The first is the sermon; the second is the mid-size learning community; the third is the small group; the fourth is the weekly study guide, which contains a daily reading, study and application component; and the fifth is the specialized classes available during the week at the church. Few people exploit all of these opportunities every single week, but the concept of tying together so many interwoven elements that guide the persona along an intentional developmental path, with a similarly integrated and focused assessment instrument, is unique and effective.

This model does not use events. It also minimizes other church programs and specialized ministries in favor of accomplishing all ministry through these existing avenues.

Pros and Cons

One of the major benefits of this model is its use of an objective and focused measurement strategy that is the total responsibility of the individual believer. Linking the entire ministry to a defined set of core competencies also makes something that becomes amorphous – e.g., biblical truth, spiritual development, life transformation – tangible and addressable. The measurement process, combined with the 30 competencies, provides congregants with a more extensive sense of belonging and purposeful community. The aggregate integration of all ministry aspects at the church sharpens the entire ministry effort and promotes more efficient spiritual growth on both a personal and corporate level. The integration of content across all public venues and ministries also means that there is a built-in incentive to track with the worship services: missing a weekend makes it difficult to keep up with the process.

The primary concerns related to this model emanate from the foundational tool, the Christian Life Profile. One concern is the reality of limiting evaluation of one's performance in a core competency to four measurement questions: can your integrity, or love or humility really be assessed in just four queries? There is tremendous value in being able to examine personal maturity specifically and quantitatively, but you have to wonder if the instrument is sufficiently comprehensive or sensitive to do justice to a person's development.

Second, the "one another assessment," in which a person's peers from the small group evaluate his/her virtues, is of questionable validity. The concept is reasonable, but the accuracy of such measures is suspect. (For instance, do three people in your small group have enough exposure to your life to accurately rate how well you follow the Ten Commandments? Do they spend enough time observing your life to know if you always put decisions before God when pressure hits?)

Finally, this process raises the challenge of how to handle success. The more mature a person becomes, the more aware they are of their frailties in that area of development. Consequently, their self-assessment scores may decline at the very same time that their maturity is increasing. This could have the effect of discouraging believers or causing them to focus on a spiritual dimension of their life that is not as underdeveloped as a dimension that achieved a higher score precisely because the person was too underdeveloped in that dimension to realize the extent of his/her weakness.

2. The Missional Model

This approach is a blend of components found in other models described here, specifically the Competencies and Worldview models. This model was not developed with those in

111

mind, but evolved after experimentation and philosophical fine-tuning. The similarity to the other effective models is, of course, no accident: shaping people's lives requires certain emphases, as found in this and the other models described here.

I've labeled this the "missional model" – it is my name for their process, not a name they have adopted – because their approach is so closely tied to the church's mission. Their mission is to help people become spiritually mature as manifested in six core qualities or competencies. Those are:

1. being passionately committed to Jesus Christ
2. evaluating everything in their life according to biblical standards
3. being deeply committed to having a healthy family
4. being morally pure
5. being evangelistically bold
6. being socially responsible and impactful.

To facilitate such disciples, this model begins by introducing people to the fundamentals of the faith, through a class that meets at the church for eight consecutive Sunday evenings. During that run of the class, the participants form various small groups (usually 10 to 14 people) and also have their introduction to the Personal Development Plan (PDP). This tool is instrumental in helping people determine which of the six outcomes they want to focus on, what they will do during the coming year to achieve those outcomes, and how they can be measured. (The church calendar is developed a year in advance so that people can create a stable plan of activity.) Once the plan has been developed, the individual shares it with the people in his/her small group. The group then upholds each other throughout the year in their efforts to grow in their areas of emphasis.

Small groups are the focal point of personal growth. As such, every person who becomes a member/adherent of the church is required to be in a small group. The groups meet every other week. Every individual in each group is responsible for developing and implementing a PDP. Groups are typically formed around common life stages or "season of life" such as groups for singles, for young marrieds without children, for parents with young families, and for empty nesters.

To address the issue of burnout, the model incorporates two types of groups: standard small groups, geared to personal development, and ministry groups, which are geared to external service and outreach. The model thus far has found that people last about three years in the personal growth groups and then tend to flow into the service-driven groups. It is in the outreach-oriented groups that people use their spiritual gifts to a great extent to serve within the church or the community or to address social issues from a faith perspective.

In addition to the small groups, the church provides a menu of specialty classes that are intimately related to the six core, missional qualities. Some of the classes are expositional teaching, some are theological in nature, and some are practical or skill-oriented. There are no Sunday school classes or mid-sized congregations involved in this model. Special events are occasionally used to supplement the content and experiences people receive in their small group or from special classes. By the way, every specialized ministry within the church is hooked in to the missional objectives. The preaching on weekends is worldview-oriented, but not particularly tied to the activities of groups.

This process is implemented starting in the first grade. Teachers identify specific objectives from the missional outcomes that will be accomplished by each student during the year and the classroom and youth group activities are then developed around that objective. As the kids enter their teen years they are encouraged to be involved in small groups and to be plan-directed.

Pros and Cons

One of the most appealing aspects of this model is its simplicity. It takes planning, anticipation, resources and a clear mission, but the process itself is easy for everyone to understand and implement. Another advantage is that this approach is self-directed. Once people have been walked through the process of developing their PDP, and have been enveloped in a small group, they are essentially responsible for their own growth. There are small group leaders and other process managers who track progress and keep the momentum flowing, but the burden is mostly on the shoulders of the church members to make this process work. The PDP itself is a very positive tool for focusing attention and mandating people to define measurable outcomes to which they are committed. The other boon to this model is the fact that the missional objectives permeate everything within the ministry. Those elements are few enough in number to be manageable; specific enough to be measurable; and compelling enough to be marketable to congregants.

The model does not place as much weight on exposing everyone to core theological foundations as do some other models. The introduction they receive is solid but brief; they will be exposed to additional related insights over time, through the courses, sermons and discussions to which they are exposed, but that process is not as central as in a few of the other models. And even though there is great freedom and wisdom in having people responsible for their personal growth evaluation, there will be the tendency of some people to exploit the subjective nature of those assessments to get by without truly pushing themselves.

3. The Neighborhood Model

Once again, this process is a combination of elements seen in the Worldview, Competencies, and Missional models, although it was developed independently of those approaches. And, again, the name of this model is employed in this book for descriptive purposes, but it is not a title recognized by the church that created the model.

Here's how this one works. People new to the church might attend an inquirer's class to gain a general overview of the church. Once they decide they want to get serious about involvement, they would join a Neighborhood Congregation, which is a group of 15 to 20 people from the same general geographic location. That group will meet twice each month: one meeting would focus upon worship, teaching and fellowship, the other meeting would be more open for members to invite guests but would still focus on fellowship. Members can invite guests to either meeting (whenever they can get somone to fit it into their schedule). The group is led by a lay pastor who has received extensive training, including an intensive 10-week training session (complete with qualifying tests, classroom teaching, textbooks, written tests, oral examinations, and other hoops). The Neighborhood Congregation is the church's primary delivery point for spiritual nurture and care. It is also the main launching pad for casting the vision for outreach opportunities. Multiple Neighborhood Congregations are linked together for outreach activities such as a concert at the church.

Members of the geographic units are then encouraged to get involved in a more intensive discipling environment by joining a disicpleship team. Each discipler will lead 5 to 9 individuals, of the same gender, through the developmental process. The focus of those efforts will be two-fold. First, each participant begins the year by creating a personal life plan. The plan defines the person's mission, vision, values, goals and schedule for pursuing desired growth outcomes. That plan also identifies how the individual will strive to mature in five specific areas: Bible knowledge, practical ministry skills, outreach, prayer, and accountability.

Second, the disciples will be led through the church-authored discipleship curriculum, which runs on a three-year cycle, divided into six 6-week modules per year. (The ministry year coincides with the academic year: September through May.) The disciplers are trained in how to lead the curriculum on a week-by-week basis, with leadership training occurring Sunday mornings at the main campus, prior to the worship services. Consequently, every discipleship group is covering the same material in a given week. At the end of each ministry season, discipled individuals re-evaluate their growth in accordance with their pre-set goals.

To facilitate impact and the efficient use of human resources, individuals being discipled sign a covenant that commits them to one year of participation. They may choose to return after the year expires, but their discipler, based on how well they satisfied the commitment made, must approve their return. Once a person has gone through the three-year curriculum cycle, they are expected to graduate from being discipled to becoming a discipler of others. A key component of the disicpleship model is that it takes a systematic and practical approach to theology, alternating between the two each six weeks. A heavy emphasis is placed on modeling evangelism.

Generally speaking, the sermons in the weekend worship services provide people with biblical content but are not aligned with the small group content. This model makes no use of Sunday school classes, although any classes that exist may be used to move people into the discipleship process. Special classes are typically offered throughout the year, giving people a chance to take highly focused classes on specialized theological topics. In-house events are also scheduled throughout the year to both recruit more disciples and to provide ministry skills (e.g., evangelism training).

Pros and Cons

This model covers the bases of both in-reach and outreach. The standardized three-year curriculum guarantees that the church can manage the flow of content and deliver an intentional biblical worldview tableau for people to examine. The inclusion of the personal life plan at the front end of the discipleship process appropriately places the responsibility for growth on the shoulders of the laity. That plan narrows each participant's focus onto the specific outcomes that the model embraces. This model also provides excellent front-end and on-going training of leaders to perform their duties.

One disadvantage of this model includes the time commitment required for it to work. In addition to the weekend worship service there are at least two additional meetings that occur during the week, plus time needed to complete related tasks and homework. The curriculum essentially assumes a fairly hefty rewrite every three years – a significant drain on church resources. The model also assumes that anyone who has completed the three-year cycle is ready to disciple other people. Given the variety of gifts, life stages and temperament types resident within the church, maturity may not always mean that a person who is competent at understanding and living their faith will also be proficient at teaching and coaching others.

4. The Worldview Model

The primary thrust of the Worldview model is the impartation of biblical wisdom that leads to personal transformation. This model is designed to increase people's participation in the church, to upgrade their level of service to other people, to improve their ability to understand issues and to make decisions from a biblical perspective. The primary objective of this process is to encourage people to think and behave biblically – in other words to adopt a truly biblical worldview.

The model relies upon a two-year process that gives groups of people a thorough grounding in the foundational truths of Christianity so that they can become "established" in the Christian faith. These groups are open to anyone who wants to grow in spiritual maturity (a significant proportion of those involved are non-believers who often accept Christ as their Savior during the initial phase of the process.) Because the establishing process is so central in the aggregate ministry and life of the church, sermons are often geared to encouraging people to take spiritual maturity seriously and to enroll in the discipleship process.

The discipleship curriculum, known as The Discovery Series, encompasses four topical books requiring an average of one to one and a half hours a week in reading, study and reflection in addition to the time spent in Discovery class. This curriculum covers an exhaustive spectrum of basic theological and doctrinal issues. These include conversion, baptism, the work of the Holy Spirit, prayer, church involvement, Satan, the nature of God, community, service, world impact, evangelism and apologetics. The class is dialogical rather than lecture-driven and the precepts are embraced through a combination of Bible study and guided group discussion, rather than accepting authoritative claims made by an expert teacher. Group members are given the opportunity to work out their questions and applications in the presence of others who are struggling with similar issues.

This model asks people to identify the issue at hand; to study the Bible in relation to that issue; to gather wisdom from other sources; to make a personal response to the accumulated information; to discuss that response with the other members of the group; and to develop personal strategies for living out the truth discovered.

This approach is based on confronting learners with dissonance – asking them to wrestle with real-world problems and to apply biblical principles to these problems. Dissonance is achieved through case studies, group discussion and service projects. In my view, the process is akin to what Christian parents do with their children: establish them in principles that will shape their values, beliefs and behaviors, then release them to refine these principles in the real world, always with a strong support base (a small group) as their touchstone.

While each person is completing the Discovery courses over a two-year period, he/she is also encouraged to deepen their spiritual maturity in the context of a small group. The purpose of these small groups is to continue to use the Bible study and life learning skills developed in Discovery to experience the encouragement and accountability of intimate relationships and to engage in community service projects. Each small group has a trained lay leader and there are also peer mentors who provide spiritual care for up to three individuals in the group.

The Worldview model also uses special events, such as "Walk Through the Bible," as feeder activities for the Discovery process. Advanced Christian education classes (such as book studies, topical studies and leadership training) are offered throughout the year, but these serve as addenda to the main thrust of the process.

This model does not use a traditional Sunday school structure and does not integrate the Internet into the process.

Pros and Cons

The major benefit of this model is that it ensures that each individual has been thoroughly led through a process of learning fundamental spiritual truths and principles, as well as receiving ample instruction in how to think and act biblically. The "Discovery" curriculum is well-conceived and practical. The process of shifting "Discovery" graduates from a larger learning group to a smaller, more intimate group for continual application, encouragement and accountability also works well.

The dominant weakness in the model is the absence of effective assessment tools and measures built in at various points along the way. Another consideration is the necessity of devoting two years to the front-end of the process before the individual is ready to move on. The conflict, of course, is that on the one hand, people's lives often do not accommodate an intensive, two-year commitment; on the other hand, providing a complete introduction to worldview thinking and the spectrum of core biblical doctrines is not likely to be adequately accomplished in less time.

5. The Lecture-Lab Model

This model focuses upon delivering content through sermons (i.e., lecture) and using small groups as the means of exploring the content further to conceive of, and follow through on, applications (i.e., the laboratory). The bottom line in this model is gleaning knowledge and building faith-based relationships that lead to godly character and Christian service. In this approach, the purpose of biblical knowledge is not to pass tests but to motivate people to live an obedient life, to bear spiritual fruit, and to persevere through the trials and tests of life. While Bible knowledge is not disparaged, it is not the primary building block in this approach – rather, it is the launching point of a multi-faceted, coordinated developmental process.

The sermons are expository, but arranged in four to twelve-week themed series. The teacher provides a message divided in two major sections: the background and principles imparted in the selected passage, and challenges as to how to live a Christian life. The ultimate goal is to cover enough Bible principles so that, over the course of several years, people have been provided with sufficient content to grasp a biblical worldview and to understand how to make decisions on the basis of scriptural principles.

Each week people receive an outline to follow in the service, along with "homework" related to the sermon presentation (i.e., related passages to read, specific verses to study, questions to ponder), and an outline for the topic-related discussion that might take place in the small group. Within the small groups, trained leaders facilitate discussion, prayer and accountability for using their gifts to serve others. One of the benefits of the lecture-lab approach is that the questions that arise in response to the sermon can be dealt with among caring peers; the utility of the information taught in the weekend services can be scrutinized more deeply and more practically than in a general presentation to hundreds of people in an auditorium. The lab portion of the model is designed to encourage learners to personalize the insights and get feedback from group members on the personal application of the teaching.

The model requires that everything be Word-centered: the teaching, the relationships, the accountability process and the service emphasis. Once the relationships take root and the group finds its stride in grappling with the teaching content, then the focus on application and accountability kicks in. Sunday school is not part of this strategy among the adults; for them, the small groups constitute the primary learning forum. Adolescents and teenagers tend to be integrated into the worship service, and are also encouraged to be active in small groups (as well as mid-week age-based youth groups).

For the younger children, though, Sunday school classes are a crucial part of the growth experience.

The small groups each have a leader who acts as a facilitator, but who answers to a small group supervisor. Each group has anywhere between 10 to 16 people involved, and meets for a 10-week period. After the ten weeks, there is a brief hiatus and then people may rejoin their group or sign up with a new one that has openings. Upon entering a group, people sign a covenant to be involved for that period.

Group leaders are assigned by the church, based on their training and qualifications. There are different responsibilities for leaders and hosts, freeing the leader to focus on facilitating group interaction and growth. Leaders are responsible for regularly submitting reports regarding attendance, major issues being dealt with and other key insights into the life and direction of the group. There are two levels of supervisors: those who oversee five group leaders, and those who oversee twenty-five leaders. There is a regular reporting regimen; regular meetings and conversations between the various leaders; and regularly scheduled training events.

Pros and Cons

From both a theological and service standpoint, the lecture-lab model is the "loosest" or most casual of the five spiritual development approaches described in this chapter. That has many benefits, as well as a few potential problems.

Among the benefits of this model are that the sermon becomes something more than a warm and fuzzy but forgettable 50-minute God-talk. Because the sermon material forms the substantive foundation of a second go-round for small group participants, the biblical principles imparted are hammered home at least twice. Similarly, by making the sermon the core content from which personal learning and applications spring, the church can insure that over a limited time period everyone receives exposure to the basic components of a biblical worldview. Further, the emphasis upon the sermon content within small groups means that regular worship service attendance becomes more important; it is harder to be inconsistent in attending when your peers, who hold you accountable for growth, will confront you for your lax commitment to sharing the basic worship and teaching experience.

By using the sermon as the lecture content, the small group leader need not be a strong Bible teacher, but must be a skilled facilitator of conversation around a theme and the ancillary content provided by the church staff. This provides for a more relational experience and one that is not so utterly dependent upon the teaching preparation and gifts of the facilitator. This permits a large church to have more than a handful of well-taught groups.

The small group emphasis makes relationships much more significant in the life of the church – which is a definite plus. It is those relationships that lead people to integrate spiritual growth into their lives in a way that makes the process less intrusive and less overwhelming than might be experienced through a more overt process. The accountability process is more natural in this environment, and this model also fosters the expectation that people will identify their gifts and serve in connection with those gifts.

Clearly the major downside of the model, but one that could be overcome without much difficulty, is the absence of any objective, broad-based evaluation system. The church does make some effort to determine how healthy the spiritual lives of believers are through head counts, ease of recruiting participants for ministry opportunities, and the usual anecdotal evidence, but a more reliable method of assessing spiritual development would enhance this model. A better evaluation method would be especially useful in relation to how well people are doing in terms of understanding and embracing a biblical worldview that drives their relationships, thinking and behavior.

Another potential shortcoming of the lecture-lab model is that it does not incorporate any type of broad-based introduction to basic knowledge about theology or doctrine. Such insights are available through occasional classes, but these are optional components that are not integral to the model. The danger, of course, is that people may enter the system without much background or comprehension of the Christian faith and have to play theological catch-up without systematic or intentional guidance in that effort.

One More Insight

While the Internet does not play a significant role in the discipleship process of any of these churches, let me note that several of these congregations do use the Net as a back-up system for individuals who missed weekend worship services. Through audio streaming of sermons and downloadable outlines and small group assignments, these churches made it possible for those who were absent, for whatever reason, to remain abreast of key information and materials.

Something to Think About

Each of these models has something unique and valuable to offer to our study of what makes a discipleship process effective. Each of these models is more sophisticated and productive than the discipleship process that I have seen in most of the churches that I have examined. Adapting any one of these models, as they stand, would significantly boost the overall quality of discipleship in America. The Church would be radically impacted by a widespread commitment to these approaches to advancing people's spiritual maturity.

But let me throw another thought into the arena for your consideration. One of the principles I witness in every highly effective church I study is that they borrow great ideas from every place they find them. Highly effective churches are less well-known for the pride of ownership of their ideas than they are known for the pride they have in the quality of their ministry. They would rather take an idea from another ministry, adapt it to their own unique circumstances, and refine it than to insist upon developing new ideas in isolation and ignorance.

Let me motivate you to follow that pattern of ministry. Here is a hybrid concept for discipleship that bears reflection. It is essentially a "best of" model built by taking the stellar parts of the five models we just explored to create a new "super model" – with all due apologies to Claudia Schiffer, Tyra Banks, Cindy Crawford and the other reigning super models.

We must start with the realization that producing rabid and mature disciples of Jesus Christ requires us to create a church culture in which the concepts and practice of discipleship permeates everything in which the church is engaged. What would that look like?

- The senior pastor of the church is an irrepressible advocate of discipleship.
- Church membership is granted only when a person covenants to participate in a focused, demanding discipleship process.
- All ministry programs are intimately tied to discipleship outcomes.
- The number of programs is minimized in order to focus the church's ministry on, and through, the discipleship process.
- All teaching in the church, from Sunday morning classes for elementary school children through the worship service and other adult teaching venues, is substantively coordinated.
- The church mission statement serves as a practical tool for identifying necessary ministry outcomes, tied to an annually updated series of goals that directly relate to the mission statement and to the spiritual state of the congregation.

The process itself would begin with the use of personal evaluation tools (as found in the Competencies model) and church outcomes assessment (as found in the Missional model). The aggregate discipleship experience would be tied to the use of those tools.

After participating in a self-evaluation and goal-setting effort, individuals would be required to complete an intensive interactive course designed to ensure that they grasp the fundamentals of the faith (as delivered within the Worldview model).

Upon completion of that activity, they would then sign a short-term covenant with the church that relates to their personal development plan for that term. Ideally, covenant terms would last for an academic year (i.e., September through May).

As part of the covenant, participants would agree to engage in several activities. Among those would be a small group that meets in someone's home during the week, perhaps every other week. These meetings would be primarily for fellowship, prayer and accountability. Each small group would belong to a mid-sized congregation within the larger congregation, akin to the Adult Bible Fellowship structure. The mid-sized groups would meet every Sunday morning and would provide both an expanded relational network as well as exposure to interactive teaching related to the week's sermon topic.

Every disciple would also be expected to regularly participate in the church's worship services and in community service options offered by the church. These options would facilitate people's spiritual development as well as the ministry impact of the church. In addition, each disciple would have a mature mentor who works with him/her on a regular basis, helping the disciple to remain focused on his/her developmental objectives. At the end of each year, disciples would evaluate how they have done in relation to their pre-determined spiritual goals for the year. Each believer would develop their personal plan for the coming year in light of where they stand spiritually and what they have learned about their spiritual development capacity.

To make the process work best, all sermons preached throughout the year would relate to a planned schedule of worldview components. The idea would be to expose all disciples in the church to the building blocks of a worldview within a two or three year window.

By the way, the same process that is utilized among adults would be used among children and teenagers. The underlying idea is to build a lifestyle of discipleship as soon as possible in a person's life. In addition, when everyone in a family is moving on the same spiritual development track, it becomes easier for the family to have a shared spiritual experience outside of church. Because it is a parent's responsibility to foster the spiritual maturity of their children, coordinating the church's discipleship track across all age groups would help parents to be more effective in fulfilling their spiritual obligation to their children.

You can fill in the cracks around this basic synthesis of ideas. Such a model, implemented as the foundation of a church's ministry, could work well regardless of the size of the church or its doctrinal leanings. And, if you don't particularly care for this model, perhaps it will stimulate you to develop your own approach to discipleship based upon the strengths of the five models we have explored.

Footnotes

[1] To read more about Pantego Bible Church, visit their website at www.pantego.org.

[2] Fellowship Bible Church of Little Rock can be explored on the web at www.fbclr.com.

[3] Perimeter has a very extensive description of their process on its website. They are located at www.perimeter.org.

[4] The Fellowship Bible Church North website is located at www.fbcnorth.org.

[5] The website for North Coast Church is www.northcoastchurch.com.

[6] These descriptions are based on my observations and interpretations of each church's model. I have done my best to comprehend these models through combinations of interviews, site visits, reading materials and other inputs. It is entirely possible that I may have inadvertently misinterpreted something or missed some elements of any given model. The fault for such oversights is mine alone.

CHAPTER 8

GO, MAKE DISCIPLES

Your church is involved in many activities and programs. A disciple-making ministry is probably among the plethora of ministries already in place. Isn't it enough just to make sure that discipleship is one of the many endeavors of the church?

Establishing priorities is one of the chief functions of a leader. Wisely choosing which endeavors should become dominant priorities distinguishes great leaders from also-rans. But here's a clue as to the relative importance of disciple-making: when Jesus began His public ministry, what was His choice of priorities? His top priority was to recruit and train disciples. Although a variety of elements were important to Him – worship, evangelism, stewardship, passing on spiritual truths, building community, serving people – each of those was incorporated into His discipling process.

In most churches we fight internally over what should be the top ministry priority – worship, evangelism, Christian education, and so forth. In so doing we have unconsciously chosen the model of James and John – asking who will be first – rather than the model of Jesus

– asking who wants to be whole. We continually engage in political and programmatic turf fights because we fail to understand that when we people become true disciples of Christ, such territorialism becomes superfluous: true disciples will integrate those functions and efforts into a seamless blend of faith-driven activity.

Does that seem ideal or idealistic? I believe it is ideal and it is realistic, based on the experience of disciple-making churches. Sure, they have squabbles, but the in-fighting is less pronounced and less frequent. When we get our priorities right, everything falls into line. True discipleship must be a priority within the Church. In fact, without a heavy emphasis upon discipleship, there *is* no Church.

If we can read between the lines of Jesus' ministry, it appears that His underlying philosophy was to make disciples now, make them continually, and use whatever resources and opportunities are presently available for that purpose, but never, *never* stop molding people into Christ-likeness. The Lord knew that when people become Christ-like, the fundamental expressions of our faith will emerge naturally.

Let's Be Real

Truthfully, while disciple-making must be a priority for you, by whatever means you select, you must enter the process with your eyes open. What happens when you make *true* disciples – not just students or group members, but real zealots for Christ?

- ✓ People's lives change
- ✓ The collection of disciples – the true Church – gains favor with the world.
- ✓ Society is changed by the disciples.
- ✓ Society experiences turmoil as a result of the Church being true to God's truths and commands.
- ✓ Disciples are persecuted.

Making disciples and being a disciple is not a complete joyride. Discipline-making is not the answer to every cultural problem that exists – in fact, an effective discipleship process may create new tensions and animosities within the culture as God's principles clash with Satan's principles in the battle of spiritual kingdoms. But the hardships that arise as a result of engagement in disciple-making are no excuse to avoid or minimize our devotion to the process and its outcomes; in fact, they are an indicator that the Church is being the Church. As long as the battle between good and evil persists, we will not experience a peaceful, loving, wholly satisfying society. However, while being avid, passionate disciples of Jesus Christ will not bring about the perfect society, the thrust to be true disciples *is* the answer for each of us, individually, in the quest to become pleasing and honorable people in God's eyes.

We cannot help but have a positive impact on the world when we are being Christ-like, even though the results of our life may not always look pretty. Not even Jesus, the Son of God, the Prince of Peace, the Savior of Humankind, was loved by all people. If we follow His ways and His footsteps, we should not expect to be loved and accepted by everyone either. But God, the Father of Creation, was completely pleased with the work of the Son – and that was all that mattered to the Son. So Jesus is our model and that is our challenge: to gain the acceptance of the Father, by imitating the work of the Son, through the empowerment of the Spirit. The results that emerge are up to God to disentangle. That is a task clearly beyond our capabilities.

Look for the Marks

When you hire people, you study their lives to look for clues as to what they will be like as an employee. When you buy products, you study the contents and reviews to determine which products will provide the outcomes you desire. As you strive to become a disciple and to make disciples, keep your eyes on the substance of the subject, whether it is you or someone whom you are discipling.

Here's what you're looking for – and, if it's absent, what you are trying to infuse within the true disciple:

- ✓ the passion of Stephen
- ✓ the joy of the post-Pentecost apostles
- ✓ the integrity of Nathanael
- ✓ the availability of Mary
- ✓ the perseverance of Paul
- ✓ the transformation of Peter
- ✓ the wisdom of James
- ✓ the servanthood of Martha
- ✓ the love of John
- ✓ the generosity of Joseph the Levite from Cyprus
- ✓ the seriousness of John the Baptist
- ✓ the studiousness of Luke
- ✓ the humility and reverent faith of the centurion
- ✓ the evangelistic sharing of Andrew
- ✓ the character of Jesus

None of these stalwarts of the faith (with the exception of Jesus) was a perfect representation of each of the qualities listed here. Each of these individuals stood out for a handful of qualities, and presumably worked on developing other qualities that brought them into greater conformity with Jesus' life. As you study their paths to glory, keep in mind that even the models of our faith fell short of the glory of God. By our very nature, we always will; but by God's will, we must not accept our limitations as excuses to give up.

The real obstacles to becoming a fully devoted, zealous disciple of Christ are not money, time, methods or knowledge. The major obstacle is the human heart. When that changes, all else changes. Jesus frequently reminded His disciples that the problem was not one of knowledge but of character. The Pharisees had more religious knowledge than they knew what to do with but they lacked the character to apply it in ways that transformed themselves and their world. Judas spent many months living with Jesus, observing His ways and His miracles, learning timeless and transforming principles directly from the lips of the Master, and yet all of His knowledge and experience could not compensate for a wicked heart. A disciple is a person of Christian character. Just as Paul instructed his young disciple Timothy, if you develop appropriate character, the rest will follow.

Go, Therefore...
Be a true disciple. Go and make disciples.
And what will it look like, when it works?

True discipleship produces holistic personal transformation, not mere assimilation into a community of church members.

True discipleship is witnessed by people who are determined to be a blessing to others – people who are never content to simply accept and enjoy God's blessings to them.

True discipleship creates Christians who aggressively pursue spiritual growth rather than passively experience spiritual evolution.

True discipleship spawns individuals who develop renewed lifestyles instead of believers who mechanically check off completed assignments on a developmental agenda.

True discipleship results in people who are more concerned about the quality of their character than the extent of their knowledge.

True discipleship builds churches known for their culture of love, commitment and service rather than for their events, information and programs.

True discipleship facilitates people devoted to a lifelong journey to imitate Jesus Christ, rather than the completion of a short-term regimen of tasks and responsibilities.

Do you passionately want to become a zealous disciple of Jesus Christ? Are you committed to bring others with you on that amazing journey?

Discipleship is about complete obedience to the Word of God, driven by a heart that can stand to do nothing less and a mind that knows it pays to focus on nothing else. Can we fulfill this mammoth challenge? Jesus, our mentor, says we can. "I tell you the truth, anyone who has faith in Me will do what I have been doing. He will do even greater things than these..." (John 14:12)

If you are devoted to the process of spiritual growth, and to allowing God's Holy Spirit to shape you on that journey, how you end up will bear scant resemblance to what you were when you began the journey.

May your journey be joyful and fruitful!

RESEARCH METHODOLOGY

This book is based upon a number of research efforts related to discipleship and spiritual growth, and among churches that engage in effective discipleship ministry. Here is an outline of the research projects conducted by the Barna Research Group from which data the in this book were derived.

Surveys Among Adults

All of the following were telephone surveys based upon nation-wide random samples of adults living in the 48 continental states. The survey were conducted from the Barna Research field center in southern California, and interviews were conducted on week nights from 5:00 to 9:00 p.m., on Saturdays from 10:00 a.m. to 6:00 p.m. and on Sundays from noon through 8:00 p.m. (all times listed are the times in the time zone of the survey respondent). The interviews analyzed in this book were divided among born again Christians and non-born again adults. The born again adults were operationally defined as people who had made a personal commitment to Jesus Christ that is still important in their life today, and who believe that after they die they will go to Heaven only because they confessed their sins and have accepted Jesus Christ as their savior.

Survey field dates	Born again	Not born again
January-February, 1999	405	597
November-December, 1999	450	651
January-February, 2000	417	585
May-June, 2000	465	538

Surveys Among Pastors

In addition to interviewing churched and unchurched adults, we also spoke with two samples of senior pastors of Protestant churches. One survey was a national random sampling of 601 senior pastors, conducted by telephone during June and July, 2000. That survey was a representative sampling of Protestant churches and included questions pertaining to ministry to the unchurched.

The other study was among an elite sample of pastors and church leaders from congregations that are doing an outstanding job of building true disciples. The original sample list was developed from calls made to denominational executives, church consultants and analysts, and ministry specialists. From that list we then narrowed down the body of "qualified" churches to those who are doing unusually effective discipleship. That was determined by assessing the percentage of adults actively involved in a disciple-making capacity; the ministry emphasis placed upon discipleship; and the quality and quantity of changed lives that have resulted from the church's discipleship ministry. This portion of the research was qualitative and non-statistical in nature, based upon extensive interviews and evaluations of the church's efforts to make disciples. The churches involved in this portion of the research came from every region of the country; represented more than a dozen Protestant denominations, mainline and evangelical; and ran from as few as 150 to as many as 4,500 adults attending the church on a typical weekend.

Additional Research

This book draws on information from other surveys we have recently conducted, as well. Among them is a nationwide telephone survey of a random sample of 610 teenagers, conducted in October 1999.

BIBLIOGRAPHY

Arn, Win, and Charles Arn. *The Master's Plan for Making Disciples*. Grand Rapids, MI: Baker Book House, 1998.

Barna, George. *The Habits of Highly Effective Churches*. Ventura, CA: Regal Books, 2000.

——. *Re-Churching the Unchurched*. Ventura, CA: Issachar Resources, 2000.

——. *The Second Coming of the Church*. Nashville: Word Books, 1998.

Barna, George and Mark Hatch. *Boiling Point*. Ventura, CA: Regal Books, 2001.

Blaikie, Graham, et. al. *Discovering Intimacy with God: Book 2 of the Discovery Series*. Plano, TX: Center for Church Based Training, 1996.

Bridges, Jerry. *The Pursuit of Holiness*. Colorado Springs, CO: NavPress, 1978.

Bruce, A.B. *The Training of the Twelve*. Grand Rapids, MI: Kregel Publications, 1998.

Carr, Brad, et. al. *Discovering Your Role in God's Family: Book 3 of the Discovery Series*. Plano, TX: Center for Church Based Training, 1996.

——. *Discovering How to Share Your Faith: Book 4 in the Discovery Series*. Plano, TX: Center for Church Based Training, 1996.

Coleman, Robert. *The Master Plan of Discipleship*. Old Tappan, NJ: Fleming Revell Company, 1987.

Colson, Charles and Nancy Pearcey. *How Now Shall We Live?* Wheaton, IL: Tyndale House Publishers, 1999.

Eims, Leroy. *The Lost Art of Disciple Making*. Grand Rapids, MI: Zondervan Publishing House, 1987.

Hoffecker, W. Andrew (editor). *Building A Christian World View, Volume 1*. Phillipsburg, NJ: Presbyterian and Reformed Publishing Company, 1986.

Hull, Bill. *The Disciple-Making Church*. Grand Rapids, MI: Fleming Revell, 1990.

Jones, Jeffrey, et. al. *Discovering the Christian Life: Book 1 of the Discovery Series*. Plano, TX: Center for Church Based Training, 1996.

ABOUT GEORGE BARNA

George Barna is the president of the Barna Research Group, Ltd., a marketing research firm located in Ventura, CA. The company specializes in conducting primary research for Christian ministries and non-profit organizations. Since its inception in 1984, Barna Research has served several hundred parachurch ministries and numerous churches, in addition to various non-profit and for-profit organizations.

To date, Barna has written 29 books. His most recent works are *Rechurching the Unchurched*; *Growing True Disciples*; *Effective Lay Leadership Teams*; *Boiling Point*; and *The Habits of Highly Effective Churches*. Past works include best-sellers such as *The Frog in the Kettle*, *The Second Coming of the Church*, *User Friendly Churches*, *Marketing the Church* and *The Power of Vision*. Several of his books have received national awards. He has also written for numerous periodicals and has published more than two-dozen syndicated reports on a variety of topics related to ministry. His work is frequently cited as an authoritative source by the media.

Barna is also widely known for his intensive, research-based seminars for church leaders. He is a popular speaker at ministry conferences around the world, and has taught at several universities and seminaries. He has served as a pastor of a large, multi-ethnic church and has served on several boards of directors. He is the founding director of The Barna Institute, a non-profit organization dedicated to providing strategic information to ministries.

After graduating summa cum laude in Sociology from Boston College, Barna earned two Masters degrees from Rutgers University. He also received a doctorate from Dallas Baptist University.

He lives with his wife Nancy and their two daughters (Samantha and Corban) in southern California. He enjoys spending time with his family, writing, reading, playing basketball and guitar, relaxing on the beach and visiting bookstores.

ABOUT THE BARNA RESEARCH GROUP, LTD.

The Barna Research Group, Ltd. (BRG) is a full-service marketing research company located in Ventura, California. BRG has been providing information and analysis regarding cultural trends, ministry practices, marketing and business strategy, fundraising, worldviews and leadership since 1984. The vision of the company is to provide Christian ministries with current, accurate, and reliable information in bite-sized pieces and at affordable prices, to facilitate effective and strategic decision-making.

BRG conducts both quantitative and qualitative research using a variety of data collection methods, with particular emphasis upon the application of the results. The company conducts more research within the Christian community than any other organization in the U.S. and regularly releases reports describing its findings regarding the values, attitudes, lifestyles, religious beliefs and religious practices of adults and teenagers, as well as the current state of churches. That information is also accessible through the seminars, books, website and tapes produced by BRG.

To access many of the findings of BRG, visit the company's web site at www.barna.org. You will have access to the free bi-monthly reports (*The Barna Update*) published on the site; a data archives that provides current statistics in relation to forty aspects of ministry and lifestyle; the various resources produced by George Barna and the Barna Research Group; and information about upcoming seminars as well as the firm's research activities. If you wish to receive *The Barna Update* by e-mail every two weeks, you may sign up for that free service on the home page of the site.

To contact the Barna Research Group, call 805-658-8885 or write to 5528 Everglades Street, Ventura, CA 93003.

ABOUT
THE BARNA INSTITUTE

The Barna Institute was founded as a not-for-profit, 501(c)(3) corporation in 1995 (originally named the American Perspectives Institute). Started by researcher George Barna, the organization was initiated to provide Christian ministries with strategic intelligence that would enhance decision-making and ministry activity. By supplying strategic information concerning key issues, conditions and opportunities about which ministries lack necessary insights, The Barna Institute intends to help ministries be better informed about the culture and people they are seeking to influence, resulting in more productive and life transforming ministry.

Although various organizations conduct research related to faith issues, the Institute provides information that is otherwise unavailable to churches and Christian leaders. This entails focusing either on topics that other researchers have not studied (or have not studied sufficiently) or upon topics that are too large for churches and other ministry organizations to independently fund. The Institute is not seeking to compete with other information-providing organizations who seek to help the Church; it strives to complement what those organizations provide to the body of Christ.

The Barna Institute generates its revenue from Barna Associates (individuals who make an annual donation of $2,000 or more and receive special opportunities to access the Institute's findings and resources); through grants and major gifts; and through the sale of resources developed from the Institute's research. Past projects have included a study of the role of faith and churches among blacks in America; and the emergence of the cyberchurch and its affect on the nation's faith.

For more information about The Barna Institute, or how to become a Barna Associate, call 770-909-0000; write to The Barna Institute, 7657 Briar Crest Court, Riverdale, GA 30296; or e-mail us at barnainstitute@mindspring.com.